COLOSSIANS, PHILEMON

General Editor

David A. Hubbard

Old Testament Editor

John D. W. Watts

New Testament Editor

Ralph P. Martin

UNDERSTANDING THE BASIC THEMES OF COLOSSIANS, PHILEMON

PETER T. O'BRIEN

WORD PUBLISHING
Dallas · London · Vancouver · Melbourne

COLOSSIANS, PHILEMON
Quick-Reference Bible Topics

Quotations from the Scriptures in this volume are the author's own translation unless otherwise indicated. Those identified NIV are from the New International Version.

Library of Congress Cataloging-in-Publication Data

O'Brien, Peter Thomas
Colossians, Philemon / Peter T. O'Brien.
p. cm. — (Quick-reference Bible topics)
Includes bibliographical references and index.
ISBN 0-8499-3246-7
1. Bible. N.T. Colossians—Criticism, interpretation, etc.
2. Bible. N.T. Philemon—Criticism, interpretation, etc.
I. Title. II. Series.
BS2715.2.0275 1991
227'.706—dc20 90-28325
CIP

Printed in the United States of America

12349 RRD 987654321

To my friends at
St. Paul's Church, Seaforth, N.S.W.
Australia

CONTENTS

FOREWORD

The twin letters of Paul—written in captivity to the Colossian church and to the most prominent church leader at Colossae, Philemon—are markedly different from each other. Both letters, however, lay claim to a distinctive place in the Pauline library. The one addresses a threatened danger to an infant Christian community caught up in the throes of first-century scientism and cosmic speculation; the other is a personal note to that community's principal member, a Colossian slaveowner, on a matter of pressing social significance.

Both epistles reflect Paul's theological and pastoral concerns. In the longer letter he offers probably the first "apology" for the faith in defense of its central claims about the church's Lord and the Christian's liberty. The short letter of 335 words to Philemon is hardly less revealing of Paul's mind as it is brought to bear on the problem created by a runaway slave and his return to his master. Our appreciation of the apostle as a forthright teacher and sensitive pastor is enhanced by these companion epistles.

Dr. Peter T. O'Brien, author of one of the earliest titles in the Word Biblical Commentary series and an expert in Pauline studies, in this volume builds on his WBC commentary on Colossians and Philemon. Yet he is able to revisit these letters in a way that expresses in succinct terms and attractive, easy-to-read style the heart of the teaching in the letters. All readers, especially those preparing sermons and Bible studies—as well as layfolk who wish to know more on the mind of Paul—will find this book engaging their interest and stimulating their faith.

The relevance of Paul's message regarding the cosmic Christ and the social application of the gospel is clearly high on the contemporary agenda. Dr. O'Brien's book will add its helpful contribution to this concern to make the message relevant in our day and world.

Department of Biblical Studies
The University of Sheffield

Ralph P. Martin
New Testament Editor
Quick-Reference Bible Topics
Word Biblical Commentary

PREFACE

Since preparing the Word Biblical Commentary volume on *Colossians*, *Philemon*, I have had the privilege of teaching courses at Moore College in each of these two letters. Preparation for these classes has necessitated my examining both Colossians and Philemon thematically, as well as exegetically. In the process of interacting afresh with these texts, further interconnections have come to light, and these have been both exciting and personally helpful. As these parts of God's Word have spoken to me again and again, so I have used the material in preaching and leading Bible studies.

When Professor Ralph Martin kindly invited me to contribute a further book on these two Pauline letters, in the Quick-Reference Bible Topics series, I was more than happy to accept, for it gave me the opportunity of presenting in written form some of the results of this more recent study, especially woven around the major themes and topics of Colossians and Philemon. I am grateful to Ralph and to Word Incorporated for their initial invitation and their patience in giving me time to fulfill other commitments before expecting to receive my completed manuscript. I am also indebted to them for their helpful suggestions for improving the manuscript.

The topical presentation and conclusions set out here, presuppose and are based upon the earlier and more detailed exegetical work (*Colossians, Philemon*, Word Biblical Commentary, vol. 44, Word Books, 1982). Readers are invited to consult this volume for further information and a fuller bibliography on particular issues. I wish to record my thanks to Word Incorporated for being able to draw on material from the earlier work in preparation for this thematic and topical approach.

The themes and ideas presented in this volume are those which appear to be fundamental to Colossians and Philemon. I have not approached these Pauline epistles from a systematic-theological angle, although there is clearly a place for doing this. Instead, the agenda has been set by the letters themselves. If one were making a study of Pauline theology as a whole, there would be other themes and issues taken up that are not specifically addressed in these two letters, or are only briefly touched upon. The reader, therefore, will have to judge whether this goal has been achieved, and whether my linking of particular themes is consistent with the teaching of the apostle.

Issues such as the lordship of Jesus Christ in creation and reconciliation, the priority of the gospel, the nature of Paul's ministry, growing in Christian maturity, freedom from legalism, the place of prayer and thanksgiving in the Christian life, living between the two ages, and relationships within the body of Christ, to which Colossians and Philemon speak so directly, seem to be as crucial for Christians today as they were when Paul first wrote his letters to these first-century believers living in the Lycus valley of Asia Minor. There is no doubt that many of the challenges facing Christian men and women today are, in principle at least, similar to those which were faced by that infant congregation at Colossae, founded by Paul's colleague, Epaphras. As this volume goes forth, it is my hope and prayer that the apostolic teaching in these two letters will challenge and encourage those of us who, in the last decade of this twentieth century, confront similar theological and pastoral issues.

Peter T. O'Brien
Moore College
Newtown, N. S. W.

COLOSSIANS

INTRODUCTION

The Christian community at Colossae came into existence during a period of vigorous evangelistic activity associated with Paul's ministry at Ephesus (ca. A.D. 52–55, recorded in Acts 19). Paul held daily evangelistic "dialogs" in the hall of Tyrannus in Ephesus and they were so effective that "all the residents of Asia heard the word of the Lord, both Jews and Greeks" (Acts 19:10). The apostle's work was assisted by several co-workers and through their ministry in various parts of the province of Asia churches were planted, including those at Colossae, Laodicea, and Hierapolis. These congregations fell within the sphere of his apostolic ministry to Gentiles and he maintained warm personal contacts with them (cf. Col 1:24—2:5).

The church at Colossae

From the Letter to the Colossians we infer that these congregations were the fruit of Epaphras's evangelistic endeavor (Col 1:7–8; 4:12–13). A native of Colossae (4:12) who probably became a Christian during a visit to Ephesus, Epaphras was "a faithful minister of Christ" and as Paul's representative (1:7) he had taught the Colossians the truth of the gospel.

The many allusions to the pagan past of the readers suggest that most of them were Gentile converts. They had once been utterly out of harmony with God, enmeshed in idolatry and slavery to sin, being hostile in mind and godless in their actions (1:21; cf. vv 12, 27). They had been dead because of their sins and "the uncircumcision of . . . [their] flesh"—a statement which indicates they were both heathen and godless (2:13).

But God had effected a mighty change in their lives: he had reconciled them to himself in an earth-shattering event, namely, Christ's physical death on the cross (1:22). He had delivered them from a tyranny of darkness and transferred them into a kingdom in which his beloved Son held sway (1:13). They now possessed redemption and the forgiveness of sins (1:14; 2:13; 3:13).

The Colossians had a hope so secure that it was laid up for them in heaven (1:5; cf. v 23) where Christ was seated and where their thoughts and aspirations were to ascend (3:1–4; cf. v 27). As Gentiles who had previously been without God and without hope they had been united to Christ in his death, burial, and resurrection (2:11–12, 20; 3:1, 3). He was the same person praised as the exalted Lord in creation and reconciliation in the magnificent hymn of 1:15–20, and God's anointed one who was at the center of the mystery (1:27). As members of his body, they had his life within them and could look forward to the day when they would share in the fullness of his glory (3:4).

Because the congregation had received Christ Jesus the Lord as their tradition (2:6) when they accepted the gospel at the hands of Epaphras, they were to conduct their lives as those who had been incorporated into Christ. As they lived under his lordship, they were to abound in thanksgiving, grateful to God because of his mighty actions on their behalf (2:7; 3:15–17; 4:2; cf. 1:3, 12).

The picture is thus drawn of a Christian congregation obedient to the apostolic gospel and for which the apostle can give heartfelt thanks to God (1:4–6). He knows of their "love in the Spirit" (1:8), and he was delighted to learn of their orderly Christian lives and the stability of their faith in Christ (2:5).

Dangers from outside: the "Colossian heresy"

Epaphras had paid Paul a visit, presumably in Rome, and informed him of the state of the churches in the Lycus valley. While much of the report was encouraging, one disquieting feature was the attractive but false teaching that had recently been introduced into the congregation and which, if it went unchecked, would subvert the gospel and bring the Colossians into bondage. Paul's letter, then, is written as a response to this urgent need.

Nowhere in his epistle does Paul give a formal exposition of the "heresy"; its chief features can be detected only by piecing together and interpreting his positive counterarguments. Some have questioned whether these counterarguments point to the existence of a "Colossian heresy" at all. But in light of 2:8–23 with its references to "fullness," specific ascetic injunctions ("do not handle!" etc., v 21), regulations about food and holy days, unusual phrases which seem to be catchwords of Paul's opponents, and the strong emphasis on what Christ has already achieved by his death and resurrection, it is appropriate to speak of a "heresy" which had just begun to make some inroads into the congregation.

The teaching was set forth as "philosophy" (2:8), based on "tradition" (an expression that denotes its antiquity, dignity, and revelational character), which was supposed to impart true knowledge (2:18, 23). Basically, the heresy seems to have been Jewish, because of the references to food regulations, the sabbath, and other prescriptions of the Jewish calendar. Circumcision is mentioned (2:11) but did not appear as one of the legal requirements.

This Judaism, however, was not the more straight-forward kind, against which the churches of Galatia had to be warned, but was one in which asceticism and mysticism flourished,[1] and where angels, principalities, and powers played a prominent role in creation and the giving of the law. They were regarded as controlling the lines of communication between God and man, and so needed to be placated by the keeping of strict legal observances. This teaching, which advanced beyond Epaphras's elementary gospel, is to be read against the background of ascetic and mystical forms of Jewish piety (as evidenced, for example, in the Dead Sea Scrolls). It was for a spiritual elite who were being urged to press on in wisdom and knowledge so as to attain true "fullness." "Self-abasement" (2:18, 23) was a term used by the opponents to denote ascetic practices that were effective for receiving visions of heavenly mysteries and participating in mystical experiences. The "mature" were thus able to gain spiritual entrance into heaven and join in the "angelic worship of God" as part of their present experience (2:18).

Paul's handling of the false teaching

There is a build-up in the apostle's presentation in chapter 1, but it is not until 2:4 that he expressly points to the dangers facing the congregation. He is aware of the methods of the false teachers, and issues a strong warning to the Colossians to be on their guard lest the false teachers, carry them off as spoil (2:8, *sulagōgeō*, to "carry off as booty," is a rare and vivid word, showing just how seriously Paul regarded the evil designs of those seeking to influence the congregation): these spiritual charlatans were trying to ensnare the congregation "by philosophy and empty deceit." Although they had set forth their teaching as "tradition," Paul rejects any suggestion of divine origin. It was a human fabrication ("the tradition *of men*"), and in reply to it he sets it over against the tradition of Christ—not merely the tradition which stems from the teaching of Christ, but that which finds its embodiment in him (2:6).

In a magnificent hymn of praise exalting Christ as the Lord in creation and reconciliation (1:15–20), Paul asserts that Christ is the one through whom all things were created (see the exposition below), including the principalities and powers which figured so prominently in the Colossian heresy. All things have been made *in* him as the sphere, *through* him as the agent, and *for* him as the ultimate goal of all creation (v 16).

Those who have been incorporated into Christ have come to fullness of life in the one who is master over every principality and power (2:10). They need not seek perfection anywhere else but in him. It is in him, the one in whose death, burial, and resurrection they have been united (2:11–12), that the totality of wisdom and knowledge is concentrated and made available to all his people—not just an elite group.

Christ Jesus is the sole mediator between God and humankind. It would be foolish for the Colossians to be misled by the false teachers into thinking it was necessary to obey the angelic powers who controlled communication between God and man. That way was now controlled by Christ who by his death is revealed as conqueror of the principalities and powers (2:13–15).

The apostle's criticisms of the advocates of the philosophy with their wrong notions and aberrant behavior are trenchant, even devastating (2:16–23). Because of their legalism, the supporters of the false teaching failed to recognize God's good gifts and his purpose in giving them, namely, that all should be enjoyed and consumed through proper use (v 22). The things covered by the taboos were perishable objects of the material world, destined to pass away when used. The taboos themselves, which belonged to a transitory order (v 17), were merely human inventions that laid no claim to absoluteness but stood over against the revelation of the will of God (cf. v 22). To place oneself under rules and regulations like those of verse 21 is to go back into slavery again—under the personal forces overthrown by Christ (v 20). By his death he had freed the Colossians from bondage to the principalities and powers. They must not turn their backs on that life-changing event. Although the prohibitions (cf. v 21) carried a reputation for wisdom in the spheres of voluntary worship, humility, and severe treatment of the body, these practices were in fact spiritually and morally bankrupt. Such energetic endeavors could not hold the flesh in check. Quite the contrary. These self-made regulations actually pandered to the flesh (v 23).

In his reply to the false teaching, Paul expounds the doctrine of the cosmic Christ more fully than in his earlier letters. Hints had previously appeared in Romans (8:19–22) and 1 Corinthians (1:24; 8:6; 2:6–10), but a more detailed exposition is given in Collossians 1:15–20 and 2:13–15 (see below). Against the false teachers who boasted in their participation in divine fullness, the apostle's criticisms are trenchant: they are arrogant and in danger of being seperated from Christ (2:18–19).

1

THE PRIORITY OF THE GOSPEL

Recent study of the letters of Paul has quite properly given considerable attention to the theme of the "gospel." It is the authoritative and joyful message of the grace of God who calls upon men and women everywhere to repent and to enter into a personal relationship with himself through the work of his Son. The gospel is first bad news, in that it declares humankind spiritually bankrupt and deserving of God's judgment (Rom 1:18–3:20; cf. 3:23), before it becomes good news, with its word of reconciliation and God's justifying of the ungodly on the basis of Christ's atoning death.

The gospel in Paul's letters

The following is a summary of the main characteristics or aspects of Paul's gospel, as evidenced in his letters:

1. It is *revelatory* or *apocalyptic* since God's saving activity toward men and women is manifested in a new way, in the Lord Jesus Christ, and the root of this saving activity is God's righteousness which has been revealed in the gospel (Rom 1:17);

2. It is *dynamic* in character, through which men and women are saved (Rom 1:16) or delivered from the coming wrath (1 Thess 1:10);

3. It is *kerygmatic* not only in the sense that it is preached or proclaimed but also because it is dependent on and related to accepted tradition (cf. 1 Cor 15:1–8);

4. It is *normative* in that it tolerates no rival (Gal 1:6–9) and stands over congregations and individual believers. The gospel has a normative role because of its divine origin. Yet it is at the same time a liberating message, for it stands over against the restrictions of human legalism (cf. especially Galatians);

5. It is *promissory* in that it was promised beforehand in the Old Testament Scriptures (Rom 1:2; cf. Gal 3:8) and, finally;

6. It is *universal* because it speaks of the power of God for salvation "to every one who believes, to the Jew first and also to the Gentiles" (Rom 1:16).[2]

The place of the gospel in Colossians

In his short letter to the Colossians Paul draws attention to the great importance of this apostolic message. Within the space of four brief chapters he uses not only the term "gospel" (*euangelion*; 1:5, 23) but also several synonymous expressions in order to draw attention to highly significant features of this message. These include "the word" (4:3), "the word of truth" (1:5), "the word of God" (1:25), "the word of Christ" (3:16), "the mystery" (1:26–27), "the mystery of God" (2:2), "the mystery of Christ" (4:3), "the faith" (1:23), and "proclaim[ing] Christ" (1:28).

In the following survey we shall examine these instances in the order in which they appear in the letter.

1. *The dynamic gospel, the word of truth*. When Epaphras left Ephesus and returned to his home town, Colossae, in the Lycus valley, to speak with his friends and neighbors about his new-found faith, he began to teach them "the gospel" (*euangelion*), that dynamic message which focused on what God had done

in his Son, the Lord Jesus Christ. In his letter (Col 1:7) Paul suggests that Epaphras had taken some time to instruct the Colossians about the content of this gospel: the recipients are said to have "learned" it, an expression which indicates that his colleague (consistent with Paul's regular practice, cf. 1:28) had given them systematic instruction in the apostolic message rather than some flimsy outline, and that they as disciples had committed themselves to that teaching (cf. 2:6–7).

In contrast to the false message of the Colossian heretics, the "gospel" is "the word of truth" (1:5). As God's word it partakes of his character and is utterly reliable. Furthermore, the congregation had come to understand this message presented by Epaphras as God's "truth" (1:6). It was not man-made, for it centered on God's grace and set men and women free from guilt, bondage, and superstition.

A significant feature of the apostolic gospel announced by Epaphras was the Christian "hope." Both the noun and the verb "hope" often depict the human activity of "hoping," and on occasion Paul uses the terms in this way (Rom 4:18; 5:5; 12:12; 1 Cor 13:7). But "hope" can also denote the objective content of the hope, the person or thing in which one hopes. It is oriented to what is unseen in the future, the content of which is defined in various ways: salvation (1 Thess 5:8), righteousness (Gal 5:5), resurrection in an incorruptible body (1 Cor 15:52–55), eternal life (Titus 1:2; 3:7), and God's glory (Rom 5:2). Epaphras spoke to the Colossians about this "hope" and assured them that it was kept secure for them in heaven where no power, human or otherwise, could touch it. Though presently hidden from their gaze, that hope, which centered on Christ himself (cf. 1:27), would be revealed on the final day when Christ himself is revealed (3:1–4).

In a number of his introductory thanksgiving paragraphs (1 Cor 1:6; Phil 1:5; 1 Thess 1:5–6; 2:13; 2 Thess 2:14), Paul goes out of his way to stress the dynamic, indeed, almost personal, character of the gospel.[3] He does this also in the Colossian introductory thanksgiving: the gospel message with its focus on the death and resurrection of the Lord Jesus Christ had made its triumphal progress throughout the world, coming to the Colossians and claiming a sure place in their lives (Col 1:6). Just as it had produced a vigorous and increasing fruit of Christian life and testimony among them in the Lycus valley, so too it was spreading dynamically throughout the rest of the world, and here Paul has particularly in view the cities and towns, such as Damascus, Tarsus, Antioch, Corinth, and Ephesus, where the gospel had been taken by Christian evangelists.

In speaking of the gospel as "bearing fruit and increasing," he echoes Old Testament language which referred to human reproduction (Gen 1:22, 28; cf. 8:17; 9:1, 7) and to Israel's population increase (Jer 3:16; 23:3).

In the Parable of the Sower (Mark 4) the seed, which is interpreted as "the word," bears fruit and increases in the lives of those who receive it rightly. Like the seed in this parable the word of the gospel bears fruit and grows. With Chrysostom and several modern writers, "fruit-bearing" is to be understood as a crop of good deeds (cf. Phil 1:11), while the growth of the gospel points to the increasing number of converts.

2. *Continuing in the gospel.* Paul earnestly desired that his readers would stand irreproachable before God on the occasion of the great reckoning (1:22–23) when God calls all people into account. God's reconciling them to himself through the death of his Son was for the very purpose of presenting them holy, blameless, and beyond reproach before him. Accordingly, the readers are urged to remain firmly founded and established in "the faith" (1:23), that is, in the apostolic gospel. Paul's summons is to steadfastness in the face of the danger of being drawn away from this gospel. Like a building set on a sure foundation and erected with strong supports and buttresses, they are to remain true to the gospel message (*kerygma*). To put it another way, the readers are not to shift from the fixed ground of their Christian hope, that hope which centers upon the Lord Jesus Christ and is the content of the gospel.

The claim of this gospel to be the authentic message is attested by its universal appeal. No class or group is to be excluded from hearing it since it speaks of Jesus' lordship in creation and redemption. In fact, as the message about God's plan for the world, which Paul is privileged to serve as a minister, it has already been preached in towns and cities of the empire and is well on the way to being proclaimed throughout the Mediterranean world (1:23).

3. *Fulfilling God's word, the mystery*. In Colossians 1:24–29, where he refers to his mission and pastoral concern, Paul uses a number of synonymous expressions, each with its own particular nuance, to refer to the gospel and its proclamation. So he speaks of "completing the word of God" (v 25), which is "the mystery" (v 26), and of "proclaiming Christ" (v 28). His ministry to Gentiles was a "commission" given to him in accordance with the gospel-plan of God.

The content of this commission or stewardship—the task to be performed—is described somewhat unusually as "completing or fulfilling the word of God." The nearest parallel to this text is Rom 15:19 where Paul in A.D. 57 claimed that he had "brought to completion" the preaching of the gospel of Christ in the area between Jerusalem and Illyricum. This may signify not simply the fulfilling of an assignment, namely, that Paul has brought the gospel to its "fulfillment," to its destiny among Gentiles, but also the way in which he has executed his task, that is, fully, in word and deed. The shorter expression in Colossians 1:25 means that the word of God is "fulfilled" when it is proclaimed in the power of the Spirit throughout the world and accepted by faith. Like God's word of old (Isa 55:11) it is dynamic, achieving the very purpose for which it has been sent forth. Clearly this has particular reference to Gentiles since they are specifically mentioned in the immediate context (especially v 27).

The message itself which Paul was to "fulfill" is none other than God's "mystery" (*to mustērion*, v 27). This important theological term was used in the Old Testament, especially in the book of Daniel (2:18–19, 27–30, 47), to denote "an eschatological mystery, a concealed intimation of divinely ordained future events whose disclosure and interpretation is reserved for God alone" (G. Bornkamm).[4] The word "mystery" appears in Paul's corpus of letters some twenty-one times (cf. 1 Cor 2:6–10; Rom. 16:25–27). In this context it refers not to some future event that lies hidden in God's plan but to his decisive action in Christ in the here and now (v 26). Several features of this "mystery" are then set forth.

First, it is characterized by "riches" and "glory," two terms used together to point to the immense greatness of the mystery, with the latter suggesting that it shared in the character of God himself. Here was a message that was truly glorious, for in it the wealth of God was lavished in a wonderful way. Secondly, God had graciously purposed to make known his mystery among the Gentiles, that is, among men and women who had no knowledge of him, who were aliens and had no hope (v 27). Thirdly, the content of this "mystery" Paul assures his readers is "Christ in you, [Colossians], the hope of glory" (cf. 2:3, where the mystery of God is Christ in whom all the treasures of wisdom and knowledge have been stored up). While the mystery had been proclaimed among the Gentiles, it had been believed by the Colossians and as a result Christ now indwelt them. As members of his body they had his life within them. They therefore had a sure hope that they would share in that fullness of glory yet to be displayed on the day of "the revealing of the sons of God" (Rom 8:19; cf. Rom 5:2; Col 3:4).

4. *Proclaiming Christ*. In a statement where Paul describes his ministry and that of his colleagues, particularly those co-workers like Epaphras who had brought the gospel to Colossae, he uses missionary terminology and speaks of "proclaiming Christ" (1:28). The verb to "proclaim" (*katangellō*) is a weighty one occurring only in Acts and Paul's writings, becoming almost a technical term for missionary preaching since it was normally

used of the gospel itself or some element in it. So the gospel (1 Cor 9:14), the mystery of God (1 Cor 2:1), and the word of God (Acts 13:5; 17:13; cf. 15:36), are "proclaimed," while sometimes Christ (Phil 1:17–18), his death (1 Cor 11:26), and resurrection (Acts 4:2), as well as the forgiveness of sins (Acts 13:38), were the significant elements in the apostolic announcement. Here at Colossians 1:28 the Christ who is "proclaimed" is the one at the center of God's mystery, that is, Christ in you (Gentiles). He is the sum and substance of Paul's message. The public proclamation of Christ as Lord is explained and developed in the following words about admonition and instruction, for it is through the teaching and warning of every person that this proclamation of Christ is carried out (see the discussion on Paul's ministry below).

5. *The rich indwelling of the word of Christ.* In a paragraph where the readers are urged to be clothed with the graces of Christ (Col 3:12–17), Paul admonishes them to let "the word of Christ" dwell richly among them. As the Spirit of God indwells believers (Rom 8:9, 11; 2 Tim 1:14; cf. 1 Cor 3:16) so "the word of Christ" should reside among them in rich abundance, producing great blessing. The expression "the word of Christ" is here used instead of "the word" (4:3), "the word of God" (1:25), or "the word of the Lord" (1 Thess 4:15; 2 Thess 3:1). The change from "of God" or "of the Lord" to "of Christ" may have been due to the Colossian situation; certainly the present expression is in keeping with the rest of the letter with its emphasis on the person and work of Christ.

While the genitive "of Christ" might be *subjective*, indicating that Christ himself is the speaker when his word is proclaimed, it is probably *objective* referring to the message that centers on Christ, that word of truth or gospel (1:5) which came to the Colossians and took up a firm place in their midst. As such it is normative and ought to control their lives. The adverb "richly," which is found elsewhere in the Epistles to describe God's gracious and lavish bestowal of his gifts (1 Tim 6:17; Tit 3:6; 2 Pet 1:11), here describes the manner of the word's indwelling: the gospel is to have its gracious and glorious way in their lives.

The phrase "in you" probably has a double reference, signifying both "within you" and "among you"; accordingly, this rich indwelling would occur when they came together, listened to the word of Christ as it was preached and expounded to them, and submitted to its authority. If the gospel message which centered on Christ did indwell the members of the congregation richly, then they would mutually teach and admonish one another in a thoughtful and tactful way. Such mutual instruction and admonition would take place in Spirit-inspired psalms, hymns, and songs as the Colossians sang thankfully to God with their whole being.

6. *An open door to proclaim the mystery.* In his final admonitions to the Colossians (4:2–6) Paul urges them to be persistent in prayer and to demonstrate right behavior toward outsiders. The apostle, who regularly remembered the Colossians in his prayers (1:3, 9–14), requests them to bring him and his co-workers before the throne of grace, asking that God would open a door for the gospel message and his messenger, which might well involve Paul's release from prison (v 3). The content of their petition is not for the personal benefit of Paul and his companions but for the preaching of the gospel: it is that "God may open a door for our message." The image of an open door appeared frequently in Hellenistic thought and could refer to a person's being free to go anywhere or write anything.

Within the New Testament this picture of an open door, which is used in missionary contexts, denotes the provision of an opportunity (cf. Rev 3:8). God opens a door for the missionary by giving him a field in which to work (1 Cor 16:9; 2 Cor 2:12) and he opens a door of faith to Gentiles so that they might believe (Acts 14:27). Colossians 4:3 exhorts believers to petition God to open a door for the gospel message. This may also mean a door for the messenger, but here the emphasis falls upon the dynamic, almost personal, character of the word (cf. 2 Thess 3:1, a prayer request):

> Finally, brothers, pray for us that the message of the Lord may run and be honored.

Paul is concerned for opportunities for effective evangelism; and it is just possible that he is asking them to pray for his release from prison. On the other hand, even when he was at liberty, such doors did not open up to him automatically (1 Cor 16:9; 2 Cor 2:12). The apostle desires that God would open a door "in order that we may proclaim the mystery of Christ." Once again "mystery" is used to denote God's plan of salvation which is centered in Christ and has special reference to Gentiles (cf. Col 1:26; 2:2). As their apostle, Paul has the great privilege of making known the previously hidden divine purpose by which Gentiles are incorporated into the Messiah on an equal footing with Jews. He now asks that the Colossians may pray to the living God to enable his apostle to set forth that divine mystery in a clear and effective manner.

Paul's letter to the Colossians declares in a variety of ways the authoritative and joyful message of the grace of God by which he calls upon men and women everywhere to repent and to enter into a personal relationship with himself through the death of his Son. It is a dynamic and powerful proclamation, setting men and women free from guilt, bondage, and superstition. As God's word it shares in his character and is utterly reliable. This message is God's "mystery" which had been kept hidden for ages but is now revealed in the life and death of his Son. Paul speaks of it as being truly glorious, for in the gospel the wealth of God has been lavished in a wonderful way. Gentiles have now been privileged to understand this mystery; it has been proclaimed among them, and those who have welcomed it into their lives are rightly related to the living God through the Lord Jesus. God's Son now indwells them and they are members of his body.

Because the message centers on the Lord Jesus Christ, it may be spoken of as "the word of Christ" (see chapters 3 and 4 on the Lord Jesus Christ). As such it is to have its glorious way in believers' lives; they are to bow to him who is the center of the gospel and come under his gracious rule. Finally, since the gospel is universal, prayer is to be offered to God that he might open a door for the message and enable his representatives to speak it clearly, boldly, and winsomely.

This authoritative and joyful message of God's grace is still powerful today. By it God calls men and women into a personal relationship with himself through his Son, the Lord Jesus. Within this new relationship that is "in Christ" they are set free from guilt, bondage, and despair.

It is clear, however, from our survey in Paul's letters and our specific study of Colossians, that the "gospel," though described by different terms and presented in a variety of ways, is quite specific regarding its origin, content, and effects: it focuses on God's work of saving men and women in and through the death and resurrection of his Son. By contrast, in many of our contemporary churches the term "gospel" is a vague notion, used as a cipher for almost anything that may generally be called "Christian."

There is, therefore, a great need to return to this authoritative and liberating message. A church that is truly apostolic today will hold fast to and rejoice in this glorious gospel. Its members, both individually and collectively, will seek to pattern their lives after the Lord Jesus who is at the center of this divine announcement; and they will be concerned to tell others, who live in a broken and desperate world, of its divine forgiveness and restoration.

2 THE MINISTRY OF PAUL AND HIS COLLEAGUES

The Letter to the Colossians, together with its companion Letter to Philemon, throws interesting—indeed, important—light on Paul's understanding of his apostleship and the ministry of his colleagues. He was not directly responsible for planting the churches at Colossae, Laodicea or Hierapolis. As we have seen, these congregations were the fruit of Epaphras's evangelistic endeavor (Col 1:7–8; 4:12–13). Nevertheless, they fell within the sphere of his apostolic ministry to Gentiles, and he maintained warm personal contacts with them (cf. 1:24–2:5).

Paul's apostleship

Paul presents himself as "an apostle of Christ Jesus" in his introduction to the letter. This description is not in response to attacks on his apostleship in Colossae, as there had been at Galatia and Corinth (cf. Gal 1:1, 10–12; 1 Cor 9:1–3; 2 Cor 10–13), but because he wished to establish his credentials at the outset. He would expose and refute the false teaching (cf. Col 2:4, 8) that had begun to intrude into the life of the congregation, and underscore the rightness of Epaphras's instruction, given to this infant Christian community. So by the addition of this title, Paul draws attention to the official character of his writing to the community.

As an "apostle" he belongs to "Christ Jesus" and has been called to this ministry "through the will of God" (Col 1:1), an expression that is tantamount to a declaration of God's unmerited grace, as well as a renunciation of personal worth (cf. 2 Cor 1:1). This calling in accordance with the divine purpose had special reference to his ministry to Gentile congregations (cf. Eph 3:1–13). He had both the authority and the responsibility as an apostle to teach (cf. 1 Tim 2:7) and to deal pastorally with churches in his care.

The classic passage in Colossians where Paul spells out in some detail the nature of his ministry is 1:24–2:5, which has been called "Paul's Mission and Pastoral Concern." Within this important paragraph a number of images are employed in order to present different facets of his apostolic service.

1. He is a "servant" (*diakonos*) of the church (1:24–25). Having stated that he is a servant of the gospel (v 23), Paul describes his suffering and its relation to his God-given task: "Now I rejoice in my sufferings for your sake, and I fill up in my flesh what is still lacking in regard to Christ's afflictions, for the sake of his body, which is the church. I have become its minister in accordance with the commission God gave me." This is an unusual remark, and has been an exegetical enigma since earliest times, for it seems to express ideas that go beyond Paul's other statements and which seem to have no parallel in the rest of the New Testament.

Elsewhere Paul speaks of suffering as an integral part of his apostolic ministry (e.g., 1 Cor 4:9–13; 2 Cor 11:23–33), and as such was closely linked with the clear proclamation of the gospel (2 Cor 4:4–6 with vv 7–18). Paul had been forewarned of this by Christ at the time of his calling (Acts 9:16). But at Colossians 1:24–25, where he refers to his being a "servant" (*diakonos*) of the church, he states something more: "and I fill up in my flesh what is still lacking in regard to Christ's afflictions." This latter expression does not describe Christ's suffering, passion, and death—as though there was still something lacking in the vicarious work of Christ which must be supplied by the apostle. Instead, it designates the messianic woes of Jewish apocalyptic teaching, based on the Old Testament, that would usher in the end-time. The New Testament takes up this teaching and makes it plain that with the death and resurrection of the Lord Jesus the coming age has already been inaugurated. But the present age continues. Christians, living between the first and second comings of Christ, already experience these afflictions and sufferings. Indeed, it is through them that we enter the kingdom of God (Acts 14:22; cf. 1 Thess 3:3, 7). Suffering with Christ, that is, participating in Christ's afflictions, is a necessary prerequisite to being glorified with him (Rom 8:17). God has both appointed the day when the Son will return and set a definite limit to the afflictions that must be endured.

The exalted Christ in heaven continues to suffer in his members, not least in Paul himself. The apostle had learned this truth at the time of his conversion on the Damascus road. When confronted by the risen Christ, he was asked the searching question: "Saul, Saul, why do you persecute *me?*" (Acts 9:4). His wreaking havoc in the church and causing the Christians to suffer was nothing less than persecuting Christ himself. Jesus had already taught this truth to his disciples (cf. John 15:18–21). Now as a "servant" of the church, Paul's sufferings are not only for Christ's sake; they are also a participation in "Christ's afflictions" (cf. Phil 3:10), and he rejoices in this privilege. Because he suffers in the carrying out of his service as an apostle to Gentiles, it can be said that he suffers on behalf of the Colossian Christians and other Gentiles like them. God has set a definite limit to these messianic woes, these afflictions of Christ; therefore, the more Paul bears in his own person, the less the Colossians need to as they enter the kingdom of God. And for

Paul and the Colossians alike, neither these nor any other afflictions can separate them from the love of God in Christ Jesus our Lord (Rom 8:38–39).

2. Paul is a "steward" who dispenses the word of God, i.e., the mystery previously hidden (Col 1:25–27). We have already examined this passage in relation to the issue of the gospel's priority (see above) and noted that the apostle has used a number of synonymous expressions to refer to this authoritative message and its proclamation. Verse 25 speaks about the *oikonomia* ("commission") that God has given him. He is a steward (1 Cor 4:1) who has been entrusted with this commission (1 Cor 9:17). He is not able to withdraw from this solemn responsibility, but must fulfill it obediently. As a steward of the mysteries of God it is expected of him that he be found trustworthy (1 Cor 4:2). His stewardship is part of God's plan (cf. Eph 1:10; 3:2, 9–10) and its content, that is, the task to be performed, is that of fulfilling the word of God.

3. Paul describes himself (and his co-workers like Epaphras) as an "evangelist-teacher" with clear-cut goals (v 28). He was a vigorous missionary who proclaimed Christ as the center and content of the mystery (*katangellō*, "proclaim," is almost a technical term for missionary preaching). His proclamation was effected by "admonishing and teaching everyone with all wisdom," as the following words show. Paul was not satisfied with some superficial presentation of the saving message of Christ to the world; consequently he systematically warned and taught men and women in pastoral situations as he "placarded" Jesus Christ as Lord (the two verbs "warning" and "teaching" are present continuous tenses).

Further, by emphatically repeating the words *panta anthrōpon*, "everyone" [lit.] "every man," which appear three times, the apostle made it clear that: (a) the evangel he brought was universal—in contrast to the intellectual exclusiveness of the false teachers—and (b) he was concerned to see individual men and women come under the lordship of Jesus Christ. Consistent with his regular practice, Paul sought to bring the word of God to bear on the lives of individuals (note especially 1 Thessalonians 2:11–12), and he no more subjected his hearers to a stock harangue than he expected of the Colossians in their dealings with their non-Christian friends (4:6, "that you may know how to answer everyone").

This model of ministering to men and women personally and individually (cf. Acts 20:20), was emulated by Paul's colleagues who served with him in the gospel, for in verse 28 he deliberately reverts to the plural ("*we* proclaim," "*we* admonish," and "*we* teach"). One could not have been a member of this apostolic band for long without realizing that Paul, like his Master, cared for the ultimate well-being of *individual* men and women.

As an evangelist-teacher Paul had clear-cut goals, a point which is made in the final clause of verse 28 where the purpose of his Christ-centered instruction is stated: "in order that we may present every person perfect in Christ." As a true pastor, Paul was aware of the real progress in faith and love (1:4) which the Colossians had made; yet he will not be satisfied with anything less than their full Christian maturity on the final day. Hence, all his evangelistic and teaching activities were directed to this end. Furthermore, this eminently worthy goal was perfectly in line with the purposes of God. The apostle has just stated that the Father's intention in reconciling men and women to himself through the mighty work of his Son on the cross was in order to present them holy, blameless, and irreproachable before him on the final day (1:22). That divine purpose is precisely the same as the goal of Paul's ministry: the perfection of each one in Christ at the Parousia (Rom 14:10).

4. Considering the prospect of their full completeness in Christ, Paul speaks of his ministry as that of an "athlete" or "contestant" which required the maximum effort (Col 1:29). He expended all his energies in the exercise of this ministry. His apostolic tasks were not finished with the conversion of

men and women to Christ. This was but the beginning and his work would only be complete on the day of Christ (cf. Phil 1:6); then the quality of his ministry, as evidenced in the lives of his converts, would be tested (Gal 2:2; Phil 2:16). Using first a term taken from secular Greek that came to describe severe labor (*kopos*), and then an even stronger word employed to denote either a physical conflict in which weapons were used or an athletic contest (*agōnizomai*, from which the English "agony" and "agonize" are drawn), Paul focuses on the intense striving and effort needed to fulfill the goal of presenting each one fully mature in Christ. Yet he gladly acknowledged that the strength for such unremitting labor came from above. As he earnestly expended all his energies in the prosecution of his apostolic tasks, he knew that the God who had shown his almighty power by raising Christ from the dead was now working mightily in and through his own life. Paul was enabled to work energetically because the God who now works supernaturally in the lives of his people enabled him to do so. The energizing dynamic of divine power was more than adequate for the needs of Paul's high calling.

It was because of this God-given ministry as a "servant" of the church, a "steward" who dispenses the word of God, an "evangelist-teacher" with clear-cut goals, and an "athlete" or "contestant" who works so energetically, that Paul was striving so mightily on behalf of the Christians at Colossae, Laodicea, and Hierapolis. Though not able to visit them (2:1), he maintained warm personal contacts with them (his sufferings are "for your sake," 1:24; his commission was "to you," v 25; he is "for you . . . and for all who have not seen my face," 2:1; and although absent in body, he is present in spirit, 2:5). Paul's earnest ambition was that the readers might be strengthened and instructed so that they would come to know more of Christ in whom all the treasures of wisdom and knowledge are hidden, and thus be able to combat the pernicious teaching that was seeking to invade the congregation.

The ministry of Paul's colleagues

Throughout most of his apostolic service Paul was surrounded by a band of co-workers whom God had chosen to labor in the gospel with him. Several of these colleagues, like Epaphras, worked with Paul in a particular geographical area. The ministry of others, especially Timothy, spanned a longer period of time, and was not limited to one place.

In all of Paul's letters some mention or other is made of these co-workers. Even the Letter to the Romans, written to a congregation which neither Paul nor any of his colleagues had founded, makes extensive reference to friends and fellow-workers who had served with him in the gospel (Rom 16). The Letter to the Colossians is no exception and provides us with a number of insights into the relationships Paul had with these Christians who ministered alongside him.

1. *Timothy*. This valued colleague is the first mentioned in the letter, for Paul associates his name with his own in the salutation (Col 1:1; Philem 1; cf. 2 Cor 1:1; Phil 1:1; 1 Thess 1:1; 2 Thess 1:1). He was in Paul's company for much of his Ephesian ministry. Judging by the tributes the apostle pays to him elsewhere (1 Thess 3:2; 1 Cor 4:17; and especially Phil 2:19–24) it is clear that of all those who were associated with Paul's missionary activity none held a more honored place than Timothy. He is described as a "brother," which in this context signifies not so much "fellow-Christian" as "co-worker" or "helper." The mention of his name suggests Paul was not alone in his imprisonment but had this valued colleague alongside him as he wrote his letter.

2. *Epaphras*. We have already referred to Epaphras as the evangelist and church-planter of Colossae who paid Paul a visit in Rome and informed him of the state of the churches in the Lycus valley (Col 1:7–8). As a "minister (*diakonos*) of Christ," he was one of a special class of co-workers active in preaching and teaching (cf. 1 Cor 3:5). He had been Paul's representative

in Colossae and had discharged his responsibilities faithfully (*pistos*). Indeed, the presence of three flourishing congregations in the Lycus valley, namely Colossae, Laodicea, and Hierapolis, testified to the enduring quality of Epaphras's work. Paul calls him a "beloved fellow-servant" (v 7) thereby drawing attention to his reliable associate who had taught the true apostolic gospel to the Colossians.

The apostle goes out of his way to stress the close connection between his own ministry and that of Epaphras. Both were involved in the same struggle for the gospel (4:12). Both were committed to urgent intercessory prayer as part of that struggle (cf. 1:9–11), while both were concerned for the full-blown maturity of the Christians at Colossae and in the Lycus valley generally (1:28–29; 2:1–5; 4:12).

3. *Tychicus*. As the messenger who will take this letter to the Colossians and give them all the news about Paul, Tychicus may well have been Paul's special envoy at this time to the churches of provincial Asia which had been established during the apostle's Ephesian ministry. The letter itself does not give the readers many details about Paul's situation, but Tychicus along with Onesimus (see below) will be able to remedy this lack. At the same time, this colleague and co-worker, who is commended as a "beloved brother and faithful minister and fellow-servant in the Lord," will be able to impress the apostle's teaching on the congregation and strengthen them (4:7–9).

4. *Other colleagues*. In his list of final greetings (4:7–18) Paul mentions in passing a number of other colleagues and co-workers. These include Aristarchus (v 7), Mark, the cousin of Barnabas (v 7), and Jesus Justus (v 11), all of whom were Jewish Christians. During the two years of Paul's imprisonment in Rome, these faithful co-workers for the kingdom of God had proved to be a great comfort to him. But nothing else is said about their ministry or that of Luke and Demas.

Archippus, a member of the congregation at Colossae, is urged to "complete the ministry you have received in the Lord"

(4:17). Precisely what this is we are not told. Paul, in Philemon 2, calls him "our fellow-soldier," and this description is employed elsewhere in a figurative sense for those who devote themselves to the service of the gospel (Phil 2:25). He was a member of Philemon's household, perhaps even Philemon and Apphia's son, who may have been involved in the ministry of preaching. (On Philemon's ministry and his relationship with Paul, see chapter 8.)

3

THE PERSON AND WORK OF THE LORD JESUS CHRIST

When the apostle put pen to paper to warn the Colossian Christians of the dangers of the heretical teaching that was threatening the integrity of the congregation, he launched a strident attack on the methods and errors of the false teachers (Col 2:8–23). But Paul did not stop with his criticisms of the "heresy." On the positive side he proceeded to set forth some of the most profound teaching in the New Testament on the person and work of the Lord Jesus Christ. For this reason it has sometimes been suggested that the Letter to the Colossians contains the "highest Christology of all."

In a section which functions as a pivotal passage (2:6–7), Paul sets forth positive instruction which serves as a basis for his attack on the Colossian heresy and in the process he summarizes much of what has preceded. Reflecting at least on their personal commitment to Christ when they accepted the gospel at the hands of Epaphras, Paul speaks of the readers having received "Christ Jesus the Lord" as their tradition. What may be said about this one whom they have received? He is none other than Christ Jesus who is the Lord of all, in both creation and reconciliation (1:15–20), and who is at the center of the mystery (1:27; 2:2).

In order to gain a fuller picture of the apostle's teaching about the person of Christ, it is necessary to survey his references in the letter and draw together the main threads. A separate treatment of 1:15–20 follows.

The titles used of Jesus

The designation Paul uses more frequently than any other in the Letter to the Colossians when he speaks of the most important person in his life is "Christ" (the term by itself: 1:7, 24, 27–28; 2:2, 5, 8, 11, 17, 20; 3:1 [twice], 3–4, 11, 15–16; 4:3). He uses it both with and without the article, i.e., "Christ" or "the Christ"—apparently with no difference in meaning. "Christ Jesus" turns up on three occasions (1:1, 4; 4:12), while "the Lord Christ" is used once (3:24). The fuller title "the/our Lord Jesus Christ" appears twice (1:3; 2:6), and the designation "Lord" is used of Jesus some nine times (1:10, especially in the household code: at 3:18, 20, 22–24; 4:1, 7, 17). Colossians 1:13 calls Jesus the "Son whom God loves."

Who is this Lord Jesus and what has he done?

When we ask the question: Who is this Lord Jesus Christ at the center of Paul's life? the Letter to the Colossians provides us with an extensive, though not necessarily detailed, response. At one level Paul bears testimony to a high Christology by asserting that in Christ whom he serves "all the fullness of deity dwells in bodily form" (Col 2:9). The one in whom Paul and his friends at Colossae are complete is Lord and Master of every power and authority (2:10). He is "Head" over all principalities and powers, for God has divested them of all authority in him (2:15). Further, and in contrast with the divisions that separate people in the world, Paul triumphantly concludes that "Christ is all and in all" (3:11). He is absolutely everything or all that matters, and he indwells all the members of the new humanity, regardless of race, class, or background. Also, he is the beloved Son who holds sway over his own kingdom in which redemption and the forgiveness of sins are to be found (1:13–14).

Paul's teaching about the person of Christ Jesus is often presented in relation to his own (and others') ministry (see chapter 2). He writes his letter as one who is an apostle "of Christ Jesus" (1:1), that is, as one who belongs to his Lord and has been called to his ministry through the will of God, an expression that declares God's unmerited grace and is a renunciation of personal worth. He expends all his energies in the exercise of his ministry which focuses on the open proclamation of Christ (who is the center of God's mystery), with the goal of presenting every man and woman perfect in Christ (1:28). Paul can refer to Epaphras as being "a faithful minister of Christ" (1:7; 4:12) and to Tychicus as being a faithful minister and fellow-servant in the Lord (4:7), while he can urge Archippus to complete the work he has received in the Lord (4:17; cf. Phil 1:6).

A significant number of references to the Lord Jesus Christ in this letter focus on the motif of spiritual union, that is, they have to do with being "in Christ" or "in the Lord." So Paul addresses his letter to the faithful brothers and sisters who are "in Christ" (1:2). They are those who live under the lordship of Christ for they have been brought into a living fellowship with him. When Paul speaks of their "faith in Christ Jesus" (1:4), he is thinking not of his Lord as the object to which their faith is directed but as the one who is the sphere in which their faith is lived out.

In a paragraph (2:9–15) where the motif of incorporation ("in Christ" or "in him") runs like a scarlet thread, Paul makes it obvious that it is in union with Christ alone that the readers have fullness of life (v 10). He elaborates on what this means by describing their participation in Christ's death, burial, and resurrection. So it is in Christ that they were circumcised with a circumcision not made with hands, that is, spiritually speaking, they died with Christ in his death (v 11), it was in him that they were buried together, and with him that they were raised from the dead (v 12). God had made them alive with Christ when they were dead because of their sins and their sinful nature, effecting a mighty victory over the principalities and powers whom he had led in triumphal procession "in him" (v 15).

Like a conquering Roman general who has won a mighty victory over his enemies and now leads them in a tumultuous procession through the streets of Rome to celebrate the fruits of his victory, God has, in the death of his Son, defeated and disarmed the evil spiritual powers that had held men and women in bondage. He has freed them from their trespasses and sins and given them new life in his Son.

Continuing this motif of being "in Christ," the apostle writes of the readers' having died with Christ to the principalities of this world (2:20; cf. 3:3), of their having been raised with Christ (3:1), with their new life now hidden in Christ with God (3:3), so that when he will appear they, too, will appear with him in glory (v 4). Indeed, so central is Christ Jesus to the life of the Christian that if any false teacher persists in his erroneous ways, he is in danger of losing contact with Christ the Head who is the source of life and nourishment for the whole body (2:19).

Accordingly, the Lord Jesus Christ is the person under whose rule and in accordance with whose character the whole of life is to be lived. In becoming a Christian, the believer calls upon Jesus as Lord and comes under his authority (Rom 10:9–10). He belongs wholly to this Lord; everything he says or does should reflect this fact. Thus, Paul prays that the Colossians may live a life "worthy of the Lord and please him in every way" (1:10). It is "in the name of the Lord Jesus" that everything, whether in word or deed, is to be done and through him that thanks are to be given to the Father (3:17; contrast 2:8). This comprehensive injunction at the climax of an exhortatory section leads into the household table of 3:18–4:1 where the lordship of Jesus over the whole of life is clearly stated. No area of family affairs or work stands outside his control and the household rules indicate how obedience to him is concretely expressed. A life ruled from above where Christ is reigning is a life in marriage, parenthood, and everyday work. Commands are furnished with the motivation "in the Lord." The readers are admonished to do what is "proper in the Lord" (3:18) or "is pleasing in the Lord" (v 20). Paul reminds them of the fear of the Lord (v 22), and their conduct is regarded as done for the Lord (v 23). Reference is made to the Lord's judgment (vv 24–25; 4:1), while they are admonished to "serve the Lord Christ" (3:24). This Lord Jesus provides the motivation for all that they are to be and to do in Christ. The whole of life, thought, and conduct of believers is to be submitted to the lordship of Jesus Christ.

Because of their identification with Christ—the new humanity—the readers are urged to put on the graces of Christ (3:11–14). They are to don the very clothing (attributes) of the Lord Jesus, articles such as compassion, kindness, humility, gentleness, and patience, and this will involve forgiving one another just as the Lord has forgiven them (3:13). They are also to let Christ's peace hold sway over every aspect of their lives as they relate to one another (3:15); in other words, Christ himself, who is the Lord of peace, is to be present and ruling in their midst. Further, the word of Christ—the gospel message which centers on him—is to have its gracious and glorious way in their midst (3:16).

The death of the Lord Jesus

In this short letter to the Colossians, Paul makes some highly significant statements about Christ's death and what it has achieved. Both the contexts in which these examples occur and their specific teaching make it plain that the apostle regarded the death of the Lord Jesus as having enormous salvation significance—historical and personal. Clearly, the purposes of God for the whole universe and the salvation of humankind were closely tied in with the one who had been so ignominiously executed on a Roman cross.

The first reference to Jesus' death occurs in the final strophe (stanza) of 1:15–20 where the "high point" of the hymn occurs (see the treatment below). The universal reconciliation of which the apostle writes has been achieved through this mighty event in history, namely, the death of Jesus Christ upon the cross. The message about the reconciliation of the cosmos has particular relevance for the Colossian Christians. Addressing his readers directly ("and you," v 21), Paul reminds them of their pre-Christian past when they were enemies, alienated from God and his people. The gravity of their previous situation sets in bolder relief God's gracious and mighty action of reconciling them to himself. That reconciliation was accomplished in history by one who was truly incarnate and who really died. At great cost, God's Son died upon the cross. And he effected that reconciliation through Jesus' death with a particular end in view: to present the Colossians holy, blameless, and irreproachable before him (v 22). The death of Christ thus had as one of its primary goals the "entire sanctification" of these believers, that is, their fitness and preparedness for the final day when they would stand before him at the Day of Reckoning.

Although some have claimed that the expression "Christ's afflictions" (1:24) is a reference to Christ's death on the cross, or at least his general experience of suffering, it is rather to be understood against an Old Testament and Jewish background with its apocalyptic conception of the afflictions of the end-time, and thus the phrase designates the birth pangs of the Messiah, those woes that would usher in the coming anointed ruler of God. Nowhere else in the New Testament is the phrase "Christ's afflictions" used of his redemptive act or general experience of suffering. Instead, Paul uses the concepts "blood," "cross," and "death" to refer to that act of redemption.

A passage of considerable importance for our study of this motif of Christ's death is 2:11–15. In verses 9 and 10 Paul spells out that Christ is the one in whom the whole fullness of the Godhead dwells bodily and as a consequence the Colossian Christians are infilled in him (note the RSV reading: "you have come to fullness of life in him"). The apostle then elaborates the meaning of their being infilled by reference to the readers' participation in Christ's death, burial, and resurrection (vv 11–12). He employs unusual language to describe the spiritual and personal dimensions of salvation in the Christ-event: "in him you were also circumcised with a circumcision not made with hands, in the putting off the body of flesh, by the circumcision of Christ" (v 11), which we understand to mean "you were circumcised in his circumcision," that is, you died in his death. (On the subject of the believer's incorporation in Christ, see pp. 31–33.)

In verse 13 the standpoint changes. No longer is the Christian viewed as having been united with Christ in his death, burial, and resurrection. Rather, he is seen from the position of having been truly dead in trespasses and sins in those earlier days of his paganism, but now made alive by God in Christ. Once again the cross of Christ is at the center of God's action. He has made the readers alive with Christ because he has forgiven them their sins.

In graphic language Paul asserts that God had not only removed the debt; he had also destroyed the document on which the debt was recorded (v 14). The word translated "document" (*cheirographon*) is an IOU with penalty clauses—the signed acknowledgement of our indebtedness before God. Jews had contracted to obey the law, and in their case the penalty for breach of this contract meant death (Deut 27:14–26; 30:15–20). Paul also assumes that Gentiles were committed, through their consciences to a similar obligation, to the moral law inasmuch as they understood it (cf. Rom 2:14–15). Since the obligation had not been discharged by either group, the "bond" remained against us. God had not only forgiven us all our sins. He had also utterly removed the signed acknowledgement of our indebtedness (v 14). He had blotted it out and canceled the bond by nailing it to the cross: this is a vivid way of saying that because Christ was nailed to the cross, our debt has been completely forgiven.

Before they had welcomed the gospel into their lives and come under the lordship of Jesus Christ, the Colossians, like their contemporaries, had lived in fear of evil, supernatural powers which controlled the lines of communication between God and man. The word of the cross was a message of hope in this realm, too. The principalities and powers exercised their authority over the lives of men and women by holding this certificate of indebtedness, this note, in their grip (v 15). But God had not only canceled the bond and nailed it to the cross; he had also divested these principalities of their dignity and might. God exposed to the universe their utter helplessness, leading them in Christ in his triumphal procession. He paraded these powerless "powers and principalities" so that all the world might see the magnitude of his victory. These spiritual powers had not been annihilated. In that triumphal procession they were visible. They continue to exist, hostile to man and his interests (Rom 8:38–39). Nevertheless, they are powerless figures, unable to harm the Christian who lives under the lordship of Christ.

4

CHRIST THE LORD IN CREATION AND RECONCILIATION: THE CHRIST HYMN OF COLOSSIANS 1:15–20

The singing of songs formed an essential part of early Christian worship and life, as was already the case in the worship of the Old Testament community and of the later Jewish Temple. Singing was an expression of Christian joy and a means of edification and praise. The early Christians sang hymns when they came together (cf. Acts 16:25; 1 Cor 14:26; Col 3:16), perhaps following the example of Jesus and the disciples at the Last Supper (Matt 26:30; Mark 14:26).

Early Christian hymns

Paul alludes occasionally to songs being sung by Christians: (1) Instead of being drunk with wine, the Ephesian Christians are urged to "be filled with the Spirit, addressing one another in psalms and hymns and spiritual songs, singing and making melody to the Lord with all your heart, always and for everything giving thanks in the name of our Lord Jesus Christ to God the Father" (Eph 5:18–20). (2) At Colossae, when the word of Christ has its gracious and glorious way in their midst, then the members of the congregation will mutually teach and admonish one another in a thoughtful and gracious manner. They will do this in Spirit-inspired psalms, hymns, and songs as they sing gratefully to God with their whole being: "Let the word of Christ dwell in you richly, as you teach and admonish one another in all wisdom, and as you sing psalms and hymns and spiritual songs with thankfulness in your hearts to God" (Col 3:16).

One cannot make sharp distinctions between "psalms," "hymns," and "songs" but Paul's expression no doubt included both Old Testament psalms and Christian hymns. The latter would have contained songs in praise of God and Christ, perhaps modeled on the psalter, both free compositions, like those from the book of the Revelation, and fragments from liturgies.

In recent New Testament scholarship, the term "hymn" is used rather broadly, similar to that of "creed," and includes dogmatic, confessional, liturgical, polemical, or doxological material. It is not employed in the sense of what we understand by congregational hymns with metrical verses. Nor are we to think in terms of Greek poetic form. A hymn refers to any poetical composition in honor of God or Christ, or suitable for use in a liturgical setting. Such poetical pieces could be sung, chanted, or recited antiphonally as in a responsive reading.

The criteria adopted by New Testament scholars for determining such hymnic pieces are twofold: (a) a discernible rhythmical lilt when the passage is read aloud, a correspondence between words and phrases (parallelism or an arrangement of couplets), and other rhetorical devices, and (b) the presence of unusual vocabulary, particularly, important theological terms. Some of the best-known poetical compositions in the New Testament are found in the Gospel of Luke: the *Magnificat* (1:46–55); the *Benedictus* (1:68–79); the *Gloria of the Angels* (2:10–14); and the *Nunc Dimittis* (2:29–32). Within Paul's letters the most widely acknowledged example of a hymn in honor of Christ is found in Philippians 2:6–11, while Colossians 1:15–20 is also regarded by many as a hymn. In addition to John 1:1–18, some affirm that there are short compositions or perhaps fragments from early Christian hymnody embodied elsewhere in the New Testament (Eph 5:14; 1 Tim 1:17; 3:16; 6:16; 2 Tim 4:18; Rev 4:11; 5:9–10; 11:17–18; and 15:3–4). Outside the New Testament canon one collection of early Christian hymns, called *The Odes of Solomon*, has survived.

The teaching of the hymn

At the heart of Colossians lies the magnificent paragraph of 1:15–20. Paul's prayer of verses 9–14 makes sense when followed by the words of the hymn. The language is majestic. In the opening lines the writer has drawn on a Wisdom background from the Old Testament and Judaism, applying references and activities to Christ. A variety of stylistic features has been employed in order to praise Christ as the Lord in creation and reconciliation. Some of the language—for example, his lordship over the principalities and powers—appears to touch on the heresy of the false teachers.

The words immediately following the hymnic themes, such as reconciliation, are applied to the readers: Christ's mighty reconciling work had special reference to the Colossians who previously had been alienated from God and at enmity with him (1:21–23). Other topics are taken up and applied throughout the rest of the letter (cf. 2:9). So the paragraph, which focuses on the centrality of Christ, is absolutely crucial to the epistle. It is interesting that the names of "Christ," "Jesus," or "Lord," do not appear. Each stanza begins with: "He is . . ." (vv 15, 18). But we are in no doubt as to who is being spoken about: Christ Jesus the Lord. There can be no one else to whom it refers.

The paragraph contains two stanzas, as follows:

Lord in creation (vv 15–17)

The language of prayer and thanksgiving at the end of 1:14, with its reference to the forgiveness of sins, leads into a magnificent hymnic passage in praise of Christ as the Lord in creation and reconciliation. This paragraph begins with a series of predicates and statements employed in the Old Testament and Judaism of the personalized Wisdom of God, which are applied to the one who had been so ignominiously executed only a few years before.

1. *The Revealer who is supreme over the cosmos (v 15).*

The majestic hymn in praise of Christ opens by asserting that he, the beloved Son, is "the image of the invisible God." This first title of majesty, "image" (*eikōn*), emphasizes Christ's relation to God. As "the image of the invisible God," Christ is the pre-existent one who has revealed the very nature and character of God. In him the invisible has become visible. Both Old and New Testaments make it clear that "no one has ever seen God." The Fourth Evangelist, however, adds that "the only begotten Son, who is in the bosom of the Father, has made him known" (John 1:18). A similar testimony is given elsewhere by Paul who, probably with the Damascus road experience in mind, asserts that "the light of the gospel of the glory of Christ, who is the image (*eikōn*) of God," had dawned upon him. The God whose creative word in the beginning called light to shine forth from the darkness had now shone in his heart "to give the light of the knowledge of the glory of God in the face of Jesus Christ" (2 Cor 4:4, 6; cf. 3:18). The writer to the Hebrews says much the same when he claims that Christ is the "radiance of God's glory and the very impress of his being" (Heb 1:3).

2. *The Creator.*

If "image" emphasizes Christ's relation to God, then the second title, "firstborn (*prōtotokos*) over all creation" (v 15), speaks of his relationship to the creation. The term *prōtotokos*, which was frequently used in the Old Testament to indicate temporal priority and sovereignty of rank, was employed to denote one who had a special place in the father's love. So Israel is called "my beloved (firstborn) son" (Exod 4:22). In the New Testament the term in the singular always refers to Jesus Christ (cf. Rom 8:29;

Col 1:18; Heb 1:6; Rev 1:5). While priority of time is intimated in most of these contexts, the notion of supremacy or priority of rank tends to dominate. Here Christ is unique, for he is distinguished from all creation.

Some in the early church, like their modern counterparts, argued that, as the "firstborn," Jesus Christ is the first of all created beings. The English word "first*born*" is misleading, for it normally suggests someone who is born and therefore created. But this cannot be the significance of the term here since the immediately following words emphasize that Jesus Christ is the one by whom the *whole* creation came into being: "*For* in him all things were created" (v 16). Nothing lies outside his creative act, whether "things in heaven or on earth, visible and invisible, whether thrones or powers or rulers or authorities"; there are no exceptions, for absolutely everything in creation has been made by him. The Gospel of John asserts the same truth: "Through him all things were made; without him nothing was made that has been made" (1:3). Jesus Christ is both prior to and supreme over that creation since he is its Lord.

The apostle adds that not only have all things been created *through* Jesus Christ as the agent of creation; he is also the sphere "in whom" everything has come into being. Just as God's election takes place "in Christ" according to Ephesians 1:4, so, too, creation is brought about in him. On Christ depended the act of creation; it was not done independently of him. Yet the passage tells us more: Christ is unique, for he is the ultimate goal of all creation, "all things were created . . . *for* him" (v 16). This thought finds no parallel in the Jewish Wisdom literature or in the rest of the extant Jewish materials for that matter. And it needs to be remembered that the one of whom Paul speaks in this vein had recently been crucified as a common criminal in Jerusalem. However, he had risen victoriously from the dead and revealed himself to Paul as Son of God (Gal 1:15–16). Toward Christ as goal or ultimate purpose the whole of creation, and therefore history as well, moved. Probably with special reference to the Colossian heresy, Paul asserts that even the cosmic powers and principalities, which apparently received some prominence in that teaching, were created in Christ. From the highest to the lowest, all alike are subordinate to Christ. They were created *in* him, *through* him and *for* him. Let the readers realize, then, that the principalities or powers are subject to the ultimate authority and lordship of Jesus Christ.

3. *The Sustainer.*

Not only was the universe created in the Son; it was also permanently established "in him" alone. He is the sustainer of the cosmos and the unifying principle of its life: "in him all things are being held together" (v 17). This Lord is not like the god of the deists, who having created the world then proceeded to let it run on its own. Not only did he make the universe; he is also personally and continuously involved in sustaining and unifying it day by day. Indeed, apart from his ongoing activity of upholding the cosmos (note the perfect tense "held together," *sunestēken*) all would disintegrate. The writer to the Hebrews says something similar when he asserts that the Son of God, through whom the worlds were made, sustains all things and bears them to their appointed end by his powerful word (Heb 1:2–3).

All men and women, whether they recognize it or not, are totally indebted to the Lord Jesus as Creator and Sustainer. For, not only has he made every person who enters the world; he also sustains their lives daily, giving life and breath to each one. Those who are "in Christ," and therefore know him in a personal way, should express their gratitude to him as Creator and Sustainer by living godly lives. And those who have not honored him or given him thanks (cf. Rom 1:21) are urged to repent and turn to him in faith.

Lord in reconciliation (vv 18–20)

With the mention of Christ as the head of the church (v 18), the hymn passes from a cosmological perspective to a soteriological one, from the horizon of creation to that of salvation and reconciliation. This perspective is maintained to the end of the passage (v 20) since the salvific work of Christ is of the utmost significance. The second stanza thus begins by speaking of the Lord Jesus as:

1. *The Head of the church.*

Christ is declared to be "the head of the body, the church" (v 18). Many writers have claimed, on the basis of Stoic antecedents, that here in the hymn the term "body" (*sōma*) originally referred to the cosmos. But this is unlikely. There is no parallel to such a usage of *sōma* in Pauline theology where the term appears ninety-nine times. On the other hand, and significantly, *sōma* frequently designates the church or local congregation as the body of Christ. So in 1 Corinthians 12:12–27, the Corinthian Christians are urged not to neglect their mutual duties and common interests toward one another, for they "are the body of Christ and severally members of it" (v 27). Similarly, in Romans 12:4–5, when focusing on the varieties of service the different members of the church render, Paul declares: "Just as each one of us has one body with many members, and these members do not all have the same function, so in Christ we who are many form one body, and each member belongs to all the others" (NIV). In his later letters, including Colossians and Ephesians, a logical progression appears in Paul's line of thought as he clarifies the relationship which the church, as the body of Christ, bears to Christ as head of the body.

There is no need to look for Stoic, Gnostic, or rabbinic speculative antecedents as the source of the writer's ideas. It may have been Paul himself who first expressed the church's vital union with Christ, the head, in this way. Employing the Old Testament concept of "corporate personality," and by referring to "body" and "head" as he does, Paul has indisputably made his own distinctive contribution to New Testament Christology.

Christ's headship over the church is to be understood in terms of an organic relationship in which he rules over his people in the way that the head of a body exercises influence over its various parts. The interdependent relationship among the members is kept in view, while the dependence of the members on Christ's supremacy for life and power is reiterated against a heresy that called such matters into question. Headship over the body refers to Christ's preeminence over his people as well as the dependence of the members on him.

2. *The firstborn from the dead.*

The one who is head of the body, the church, is the *risen* Christ, "the beginning, the firstborn from the dead" (v 18). The term "beginning" (*archē*) has basically to do with primacy, whether in a temporal sense (Matt 19:4, 8; John 15:27), or with reference to authority and sovereignty (Rom 8:38; 1 Cor 15:24; Eph 1:21; 6:12). When Colossians 1:18 states that Christ is "the beginning," it does not mean that he is "the beginning of God's creation" (Rev 3:14), or its first cause. Rather, as the one who is "the first-born from the dead," he is the founder of a new humanity. (In Genesis 49:3 the two terms "firstborn" and "beginning" appear together to describe the firstborn as the founder of a people.) The resurrection age has burst forth and, as the first one who has risen from among those who had fallen asleep, Christ is the first fruits who guarantees the future resurrection of others (1 Cor 15:20, 23).

Because Christ is the "beginning" and the "firstborn" in resurrection, as well as in creation, he has therefore become preeminent in all things. This was the divine intention as the purpose clause makes plain: "in order that in everything he might have the supremacy." The hymn had previously asserted Christ's primacy in creation (vv 15–17); it now mentions his primacy in resurrection. In both new creation and old the first place belongs to him alone. He has become preeminent "in everything" (v 18).

3. *The fullness of God.*

The reason for this primacy is then spelled out: Christ is the one in whom God in all his fullness was pleased to take up residence (v 19). Several lines of Old Testament thought converge in this statement: first, the term "fullness" turns up in a number of stereotyped expressions with an active meaning ("the sea and its fullness," 1 Chr 16:32; "the earth and everything in it," Ps 24:1). Secondly, similar language is used to speak of God himself (or his glory) filling heaven and earth (Jer 23:24; Ps 72:19; cf. Isa 6:3). Finally, the verb "be pleased," which often appears in the Old Testament to denote the good pleasure of God (Pss 44:3; 147:11; 149:4), is particularly used to designate divine election. Of special significance is the connection between God's choosing and his dwelling place (Septuagint [LXX] Ps 67:17). So here at Colossians 1:19 Christ is "the place" in whom God in all his fullness was pleased to take up his residence. All the attributes and activities of God—his spirit, word, wisdom, and glory—are perfectly displayed in Christ. Further, this is no temporary indwelling as the present tense verb *katoikeō* (which means to "settle [down], live, reside"), makes plain: "in him all the fullness of deity *dwells* bodily" (Col 2:9).

Jesus Christ is the one mediator between God and humankind. He who perfectly reveals the nature and character of God brings us into a relationship with his Father. Accordingly, the Colossian Christians need not fear those supernatural powers under whose control men and women were supposed to live, whether divine emanations, agencies, or the like. Neither should we be afraid of their twentieth-century counterparts.

4. *The Reconciler of everything.*

The conclusion of the final section occurs and the "high point" of the hymn is reached with the statement about God's good pleasure in reconciling all things through Christ (v 20). Although there has been no previous mention of it, the presupposition is that the unity and harmony of the cosmos have suffered a considerable dislocation, even a rupture, requiring reconciliation. The opening words of the paragraph had asserted that all things, including the various heavenly bodies, lordships, principalities, and powers, had been created in, through, and for Christ. He is their Lord in creation. What is not spelled out, however, is what has happened to all things *since* creation.

The language of reconciliation is usually applied to persons. One may indeed speak of reconciling a bank statement, or of the reconciliation of propositions in the field of logic. But normally reconciliation has to do with the restoration of harmonious relationships between persons. This theme appears in four important passages of Paul's letters: Romans 5:10–11; 11:15; 2 Corinthians 5:18–20; and Ephesians 2:16, in addition to Colossians 1:20, 22. In each reference the ground of reconciliation lies in the gracious initiating activity of God (Romans 5:8 states that the basis is the love of God, while Colossians 1:20 points to God's good pleasure; cf. 2 Corinthians 5:18). The significant feature of our passage is that it speaks of the reconciliation of "all things" and this as a past event. (In 2 Corinthians 5:19, where the reconciliation of the world is mentioned, it is clear that the world of men and women is the point of reference.)

To speak of the universe as having been reconciled means that "heaven and earth have been brought back into their divinely created and determined order . . . the universe is again under its head and . . . cosmic peace has returned."[5] This notion of "reconciliation" is then amplified and explained in the following words, "having made peace through the blood of his cross," an expression that includes not only the making of peace by which fellowship with God is restored, but also the idea of pacification. Verse 20 is to be understood in light of God's triumph in Christ over the principalities and powers (2:15). However, the meaning of Christ's reconciling work should not be limited to these words of 2:15 since it is broader than the pacification of the principalities and powers: it applies to the realm of humanity, in fact, to the whole cosmos.

The peace which Christ has won may be freely accepted or imposed against the will. The principalities and powers over whom God has triumphed in Christ (2:15) are certainly not depicted as gladly surrendering to his grace but as "submitting against their wills to a power which they cannot resist"

(F. F. Bruce, *Commentary*, p. 76). In other words, they have been pacified—a concept that was not strange to those living in the Mediter-ranean region under Roman rule of the first-century A.D. This is not to suggest that with the "pacification" of, or victory over, these powers, which are hostile to God and Christ, they are immediately done away with or have been destroyed. It is evident that they continue to exist, opposed to human-kind's interests (cf. Rom 8:38–39). Nevertheless, they cannot finally harm the person who is in Christ, and their ultimate overthrow in the future is assured (1 Cor 15:24–28; see Col 2:15).

Paul affirms that this universal reconciliation has been brought about, not in some other-worldly drama, but through something done in history: the death of Jesus Christ upon the cross. The message of Christ's peacemaking work, which involves the reconciliation of the cosmos, has particular refer ence to the Colossian Christians (vv 21–23). Those who had once been enemies, alienated from God and his people, have now been reconciled to him through a gracious and mighty action, enacted in history at great cost—the death of his Son on the cross.

Verse 20 should not be taken to mean that Paul looked for the ultimate reconciliation to God of all people and, indeed, of hostile spiritual powers as well. The cosmic reconciliation has to do with "everything" (*ta panta*), and this includes, among others, the principalities and powers. They are reconciled through subjugation (cf. 1 Cor 15:28) for theirs is no glad surrender to the Lord of the cosmos. Similarly, it cannot be assumed from this verse that all sinful men and women have freely accepted the peace proffered through the death of Christ. Although all things will finally unite to bow in the name of Jesus and to acknowledge him as Lord (Phil 2:10–11), it is not to be assumed that this will be done gladly by all. To claim that verse 20 points to a universal reconciliation in which every person will finally enjoy celestial bliss is unwarranted.

In conclusion, regardless of the origins of this magnificent passage in praise of Christ (though usually ascribed to Paul) it is clearly central to the context in which it presently stands. Paul's lengthy prayer (Col 1:9–14) leads up to the hymn, while the words which immediately follow take up phrases and ideas from it and apply the truths to the readers.

We do not know how much the Colossians already knew of the language and concepts contained in the hymn prior to their receiving the letter. They had accepted Christ Jesus the Lord as their tradition (2:6–7) and in light of Paul's positive words regarding the teaching ministry of his colleague, Epaphras (1:7; cf. 4:12–13), we may assume that what is asserted in the hymn was consistent with the instruction previously given in the gospel. But we do know what Paul expected his readers to understand *now*—chapter 2 will deal with some of the ramifications of this. Furthermore, these majestic words in praise of Christ may well have become the basis for their own praises and thanksgivings, offered both corporately, as they met together, and privately.

5
THE PEOPLE OF GOD

Yale scholar Paul Minear[6] has shown that more than a hundred different terms, metaphors, and images are used in the New Testament to describe God's people in Christ. In addition to these descriptions, several activities are said to characterize Christian believers. Paul's Letter to the Colossians does not contain any systematic teaching on the theme of the people of God, as such. Nevertheless, there are important references to this subject and they harmonize with the apostle's teaching elsewhere. Further, while the focus of Paul's instruction to the Colossians is on the person and work of the Lord Jesus Christ, this naturally leads to his making significant comments about the readers' being incorporated into Christ, and the saving benefits which he has procured on their behalf. Christology logically proceeds to ecclesiology.

We have already paid some attention to what has been achieved by the Lord Jesus in his saving work and how the readers have been united to him in his death, burial, and resurrection. In this section, we propose to look at the terms and metaphors used of the Colossians as God's people. The first mentioned in the letter is "saints."

Saints

"Saints" or "holy ones" (*hagioi*) is the term Paul uses most frequently in Colossians to describe God's people. The word appears six times in the space of four chapters: five times as a noun meaning "saints" (1:2, 4, 12, 26; 3:12; cf. Philem 5, 7), once as an adjective signifying "holy" (1:22). In the opening greeting of his letter, Paul calls the Christians of this congregation in the Lycus valley "the saints and faithful brothers in Christ at Colossae" (1:2). On this occasion, the term "church" (*ekklēsia*) does not appear, but there is no special significance in this omission since "church" is omitted from the introductions of Romans, Philippians, and Ephesians; in each of these instances "saints" occurs instead. Furthermore, as 1 Corinthians 1:2 shows, the two expressions are related, for the words "the church of God which is at Corinth" stand in apposition to the following—"those sanctified in Christ Jesus, called to be saints." Although "saints" could here be treated as an adjective, thus qualifying "brothers," as does "faithful" (cf. NIV "holy and faithful brothers"), the word is usually a noun in the greetings, meaning "saints" or "holy ones."

The background for understanding this description of the Colossians as "saints" is the Old Testament. Israel was God's holy people (Exod 19:6), chosen by him and appointed to his service. Having been brought into a covenant relationship with him, Israel was to be a holy nation because the Lord is holy (Lev 11:44; 19:2, etc). Christians are "saints" because of the new relationship they have been brought into by God through Jesus Christ. They are set apart for him and his service; as the people of his own possession, they are the called and elect community of the end-time: they are "God's chosen ones, holy (*hagioi*) and beloved" (Col 3:12) whose lives are to be characterized by godly behavior.

The word "saints" can be used generally of Christians and is not limited in its application to those at Colossae. In his introductory thanksgiving paragraph, the apostle gives thanks to God for the faith of the Colossians and their love "for all the saints" (1:4). The Colossians' "practical expression of care and concern" was directed to all of God's holy people (the "all" accentuates the breadth of their love), and this refers to Christians generally, including others at Colossae, as well as those within other churches of the Lycus valley such as Laodicea and Hierapolis.

Toward the end of this same thanksgiving paragraph, Paul prays that the readers may give thanks to the Father "who has qualified you to share in the inheritance of the saints in the kingdom of light" (1:12). Although some writers have taken the expression "holy ones" to refer to angels, this is unlikely. Rather, God's people are in view. Paul's point is that the all-powerful Father has fitted the Colossians for an inheritance in the realm of the light of the age to come. "In light" goes with the whole phrase that precedes, "to share in the inheritance of the saints." Unlike Canaan, this inheritance belonged to a spiritual dimension and was unable to be ravaged by war, famine, or the like. For the Colossians, most of whom were Gentiles by birth, this was good news indeed. They now had "a hope laid up for them in heaven" (1:5). Most consider "saints" refers to believers generally, but it is also possible that it applies to Jewish Christians. Israel as the people of God had an inheritance. Gentiles, formerly without God and without hope, have now been incorporated into the body of Christ; they belong to that people of God and share in that inheritance with Jewish Christians.

The title "saints" (Col 1:26) appears in relation to the mystery of God. Paul states that this mystery, God's wise plan, had formerly been hidden. But in a dramatic turn of events he graciously made known this plan which focused on his Son, the Lord Jesus Christ. The recipients of this divine disclosure are "his saints," a phrase that refers not to some select group of initiates, but those who have heard and received the word of God, for it is in the effective preaching and teaching of the gospel that the revelation of the mystery takes place (cf. 1 Cor 2:1, 7; 4:1; Eph 3:8–9; 6:19).

Within an important exhortatory paragraph, where the readers are urged to put on the graces of Christ (Col 3:12–17), Paul addresses the members of the congregation by means of exalted titles: they are "the chosen, holy (*hagioi*) and beloved people of God." These descriptions are significant, not only because they were used of Israel as God's own possession (Isa 43:20; 65:9)—and have now been transferred to the Colossians as the new people of God—but also since they are designations of Christ (Luke 23:35; Mark 1:24; Matt 3:17). He preeminently is the chosen one; it is he who is the holy one of God, and he who is the beloved one. The point of the Colossians' similarity and identification with him is underscored in a context where they are said already to have put on the new man (3:10) and, consequently, must don the graces which are characteristic of him: "heartfelt compassion, kindness, lowliness, gentleness, and longsuffering" (3:12). Here the terms "holy" and "beloved" are parallel with and predicates of the first mentioned, "the elect of God": they are his choice souls whom he has set apart for himself and placed his love upon them.

The last reference to "holy" in this letter is 1:22 where the word *hagioi* is an adjective rather than a noun meaning "saints." God effected the reconciliation of the Colossians through the death of his Son with a particular end in view: to present them *holy*, and irreproachable before him. As men and women who are forgiven and reconciled, they are declared blameless (cf. Rom 8:33–34) so that on the occasion of the judgment they will be without fault or stain (the terms "holy" and "blameless" appear to have lost any cultic overtones here and at Ephesians 1:4; 5:27; Philippians 2:15; and Jude 24).

The church

Integral to Paul's teaching about the people of God in Colossians and Philemon (as elsewhere in his letters) is his use of the important term *ekklēsia* ("assembly, church, congregation").

This word is found four times in Colossians (1:18, 24; 4:15, 16) and once in the companion Letter to Philemon (v 2). As we examine these instances, two questions need to be asked: (1) in the immediate context, who or what is denoted by the term? That is, what is the referent? And (2) what point is being conveyed or taught through this image? The instances in Colossians and Philemon need to be set, firstly, against their first-century background and then in relation to the apostle's uses of *ekklēsia* elsewhere.

Ekklēsia appears more than a hundred times in the New Testament, and well over half of these appear in the Pauline epistles. It was not originally an "ecclesiastical" word, for it had no intrinsically religious meaning and could refer to meetings that were quite secular in character. In the context of the Greek city-state, *ekklēsia* was understood in political terms to denote the popular assembly of citizens, while in the Old Testament the word could describe the gathering of an army in preparation for war (1 Sam 17:47) or the "coming together" of an unruly and potentially dangerous crowd (Ps 26:5). In both the Greek and Jewish worlds prior to Paul, the word meant an assembly or gathering of people; it did not designate an "organization" or "society." Of special significance are those occurrences of *ekklēsia* in the LXX (Septuagint) which apply to the congregation of Israel when it assembled to hear the word of God (Deut 4:10; 9:10; 18:16).

Paul employs this Greek word, *ekklēsia*, for an "assembly, congregation, or church" in a variety of contexts to refer to:

(1) A *local assembly or congregation of Christians*. As a term which is descriptive of an identifiable object, rather than being a metaphor, *ekklēsia* denotes a local assembly or gathering of Christians in a particular place. So in 1 Thessalonians 1:1 Paul sends greetings to the Christians at Thessalonica: "To the church of the Thessalonians in God the Father and the Lord Jesus Christ" (cf. 2 Thess 1:1; 1 Cor 1:1; 2 Cor 1:1; and Gal 1:2). From the closing remarks of his letter, it is clear the apostle has

in mind an actual gathering of the Thessalonian Christians (cf. 1 Thess 5:26–27). Although Paul does not address the Colossians in precisely this way (instead, he calls them "the saints and faithful brothers in Christ at Colossae," 1:2), he clearly envisages that the letter will be read in their gathering (cf. 4:16). After this, it is also to be read "in the congregation (*ekklēsia*) of the Laodiceans," while the Colossians for their part are to read the letter from Laodicea (4:16). "Church" is here being used by the apostle in its customary sense of a local assembly or congregation of Christians.

(2) *Ekklēsia* is again employed in Paul's letters as a descriptive term—as distinct from a metaphor—of an identifiable object, this time of *a gathering that met in a particular home*, i.e. a "house-church." So Colossians 4:15 refers to "Nympha and the church (*ekklēsia*) that is in her house," while Philemon 2 points out that Philemon's house was used as a meeting-place in Colossae ("the church that meets in your house").

(3) Of special importance are the two instances in Colossians 1 where "church, congregation" (*ekklēsia*) has a wider reference than either a local congregation or a house-church: verse 18 states that Christ is "the head of the body, that is, the church (*ekklēsia*)," while in verse 24 a similar expression is employed in the context of Paul's sufferings ("on behalf of his body, which is the church"). Although most commentators interpret these references (and the similar instances in Ephesians: 1:22; 3:10, 21; 5:23–24, 27, 29, 32) as "the church universal, to which all believers belong" and which is scattered throughout the world, there are serious difficulties with this view.

First, the term *ekklēsia* can no longer have its usual meaning of "gathering" or "assembly," since it is difficult to envisage how the world-wide church could assemble, and so the word must be translated in some other way to denote an organization or society. Secondly, the context of Colossians 1:15–20, which is moving on a heavenly plane, suggests it is not an earthly phenomenon that is being spoken of in verse 18, but a supernatural one. This is not to suggest that believers have no relationships with one another if they do not gather together in church. As members of the body of Christ or of God's people, they are not only related to Christ himself but also to one another, even when separated by time and distance. But the point being made here is that *ekklēsia* is not being used of those wider, universal links.

Instead, the term is now being employed metaphorically to designate *a heavenly gathering around Christ* in which the Colossians already participate. Since they have already been raised with Christ, they are to seek the things that are above where Christ is, seated at God's right hand (Col 3:1). They live with Christ in this heavenly dimension (note that Christ who is their life is already in heaven, vv 1, 3), and they are assured that when he appears they also will appear with him in glory (v 4). At the same time, these readers are obviously members of an earthly realm, with injunctions addressed to them as to how they should go about their ordinary everyday tasks (note the exhortations of 3:4–4:6 which are examined below); further, the apostle looks forward to their blamelessness before God on the last day (1:22). To speak of "church" in this context as a gathering taking place in heaven where the Colossians are already assembled around Christ is a metaphorical way of saying that they now enjoy fellowship with him. It is a figurative manner of speaking about Christians being personally related to Christ as they are related to one another. And, presumably, further references in Ephesians (3:10, 21; 5:23, 25, 27, 29, 32) together with the important passage in Hebrews 12:22–24 are to be understood along the same lines, for they point to the same reality.

The New Testament does not discuss the relationship between the local church and this heavenly gathering. The links are nowhere specifically spelled out. Certainly the local congregation, whether at Colossae or elsewhere, was neither a *part* of the church of God nor *a* church of God. This is made plain in several places, including 1 Corinthians 1:2 where the apostle writes "to *the church* of God which is at Corinth." But we may suggest that local congregations (like those at Colossae and Laodicea: category 1) and house-groups (that met in the homes of Philemon and Nympha: category 2) were concrete, visible expressions of that new relationship which believers have with the Lord Jesus. Local gatherings, whether in a congregation or a house-church, were earthly manifestations of that heavenly gathering assembled around the risen Christ (category 3).

If this heavenly meeting with Christ is a figurative or metaphorical way of speaking about believers' ongoing fellowship with him, then it was appropriate that this new relationship with the ascended Lord should find concrete expression in their regular coming together, that is, "in church." Apparently, the responsibility of meeting together in this way was not immediately obvious to some of the early Christians since they still needed to be exhorted not to forsake "the assembling of themselves together" (Heb 10:25).

The men and women at Colossae and other centers in the Lycus valley were called into membership of this one church of Christ, the heavenly assembly, through the preaching of the gospel. They were brought into fellowship with God's Son (cf. 1 Cor 1:9), and to speak of their membership of this heavenly gathering assembled around Christ is another way of referring to this new relationship with him. They and other Christians were to assemble in local congregations here on earth, for this was an important way in which their fellowship with Christ was expressed. Further, as they came together with others who were in fellowship with him, so they not only met with each other—they also met with Christ himself who indwelt them corporately and individually.

The body of Christ

The metaphor of the body of Christ, employed by Paul to describe the people of God, is a highly significant one and is applied throughout his letters to a number of entities and with a range of connotations. In Colossians, "body" appears only three times as an ecclesiological term and in two of these it is synonymous with the "church" (*ekklēsia*): chapter 1:18, 24. The third instance is Colossians 2:19.

There is no consensus among New Testament scholars as to the origins of Paul's usage (perhaps it came to him independently), or to the precise relationship between the physical body of Christ which was crucified on the cross (see below on 1:22) and the metaphorical body, that is, the church. A number of passages shows that there is a very close relationship between the two, though not an identity. Those who participate in the body and blood of Christ, in other words share in the benefits of his death, are members of that one body.

In his earlier letters, as noted above, the expression "the body of Christ" is applied by Paul to *a local congregation* (1 Cor 12:27; at Corinth, which is not thought of as a *part* of the body of Christ or *a* body of Christ), to *Christians in their relationships* with one another—Christians who were not necessarily members of the same congregation (Rom 12:4–5)—and a wider group, possibly including *all Christians* (1 Cor 12:13), that is, all who have been united in the Lord Jesus Christ.

In Colossians and Ephesians, the "body" image is used to denote a *heavenly entity*, that is, all Christians united in the Lord Jesus Christ. Colossians 1:18 has Christ's headship over the church stated in terms of an organic relationship. He exercises influence over his people as the head of a body exercises control over its various parts. The notion of the body's total dependence on Christ for life and power, as well as his supremacy, may also be germane. In the immediate context, it is the risen Christ who is this head; as the beginning and firstborn in resurrection, he is the founder of a new humanity. A new element of growth is brought out by the body image in Colossians 2:19. In a polemical context, Paul warns the false teachers at Colossae that they are in danger of rejecting Christ as head, the one who is the source of continuous life and nourishment by which his body lives, and the source of unity through which it becomes an organic whole. (See below on Col 1:24; note also Eph 1:23; 2:16; 4:4, 12, 16; 5:23, 28, 30.)

Brothers and sisters

The last term which we examine in our study of Paul's teaching on the people of God in Colossians comes from the imagery of the family. It is the word "brothers" (*adelphoi*), which refers to both brothers and sisters in Christ. This term was one of Paul's favorites in referring to members of the communities to whom he was writing, for it was expressive of the very real relationships that exist between Christians as members of God's family (cf. 1 Cor 15:58; Rom 15:14; Phil 3:1; 4:1; Eph 6:10). Believers have been brought into fellowship with God the Father and his Son, the Lord Jesus; they are members of God's family by adoption and therefore are brothers and sisters in Christ. As an outworking of Christ's love for them (Eph 5:1–2) they are to show "brotherly love" (*philadelphia*) to one another (1 Thess 4:9–10).

The recipients of Paul's letter to the Colossians are addressed not only as "saints" but also as "faithful brothers (*adelphoi*) in Christ" (Col 1:2). The adjective "faithful" shows that they have placed their wholehearted trust in Jesus as Son of God, while the expression "in Christ" points not so much to the one in whom they have believed as the one in whom they, as brothers, have been brought into a living fellowship. The designation "brothers" is used again in 4:15 when Paul asks the Colossians to convey his greetings to their "fellow-Christians" at Laodicea.

On occasion, the apostle employs the word "brother" in a sense narrower than "fellow-Christian" to describe one who was associated with him as a "co-worker" or "helper" in the gospel. Timothy, who held an honored place in Paul's mission, is spoken of in this way (Col 1:1; Philem 1), as are Tychicus (Col 4:7), Onesimus (4:9), and Philemon (Philem 7). If anything, though, this is a specialized usage of the more general application of the term to designate a "fellow-believer."

The family term "brother" was special and precious to Paul. It was the first word he heard from the lips of Ananias when he was welcomed as a disciple of the Lord Jesus in Damascus: "*Brother* Saul, the Lord—Jesus, who appeared to you on the road as you were coming here—has sent me so that you may see again and be filled with the Holy Spirit" (Acts 9:17 NIV). Something of the deep significance of this familial word *adelphos* ("brother") comes out in Paul's letter to Philemon. As he makes his request of Philemon, Paul urges him to "welcome Onesimus as you would welcome me" (v 17), namely, as a brother. Onesimus had been a slave; now, because of his conversion to Christ as Lord, he is a beloved brother. In this sense he is on exactly the same terms as Philemon (cf. vv 7, 20): master and slave alike have both been incorporated into the body of Christ. The relationship between the two men is deepened so that, in a sense, the terms "master" and "slave" are transcended, and their behavior ought to be conducted in light of their belonging to the same Lord.

To conclude, although the apostle presents no systematic teaching in Colossians on the doctrine of the church or the people of God, several of his more important terms and images on this theme are employed; together they help to build up an overall picture which is consistent with his fuller presentation elsewhere.

The term "saints" is used more frequently than any other in Colossians and is applied to members of the congregation at Colossae, other believers in the Lycus valley, as well as to Christians generally. The term points to a new relationship into which believers have been brought by God through Jesus Christ. They have been set apart for him and his service, and this was marvelous news, indeed, for Gentiles who had been without God and without hope. They have been incorporated into the body of Christ and prepared for an eternal inheritance with God himself. As those who are addressed by exalted titles, namely, "the chosen, holy (*hagioi*) and beloved people of God"—titles used of Jesus himself—they are to put on the graces which are characteristic of him: "heartfelt compassion, kindness, lowliness, gentleness, and longsuffering."

As part of his teaching about the people of God, the apostle used the important term *ekklēsia* ("assembly, church, congregation") *descriptively* to refer to a local assembly or congregation of Christians, as well as a gathering that met in a particular home, i.e. a "house-church." On two occasions in the letter, the term was employed *metaphorically* to designate a heavenly gathering around Christ in which the Colossians already participate. This was an important way of speaking about their fellowship with Christ—a fellowship that was to find expression in their gathering together on earth here and now as they met with Christ and with one another.

Paul employed the image of the body of Christ as a heavenly entity to draw attention to an organic relationship between the members and Christ as head. He exercised authority over his people as the head of a body exerts influence over its various parts. At the same time, he is the source of life and nourishment by which the body lives, as well as being the source of its unity.

Finally, to express the close relationships that exist between Christians as members of God's family, Paul spoke of the Colossians as faithful "brothers [and sisters]" in Christ. They had been adopted into God's family and, as an outworking of Christ's love for them, they were to show "brotherly love" to one another. The family term "brother," which is generic for both brother and sister, was a precious one. It transcended other relationships (cf. Philem 16, 17) and anticipated a lifestyle appropriate to believers belonging to the same Lord.

If this clear teaching about the privileges of and demands upon the people of God were taken seriously by twentieth-century Christians, then personal relationships among church members would truly be a foretaste of heaven. In the meantime, those outside the church, seeing how these Christians love one another, may well be attracted to the one whom they own as Lord.

6
ESCHATOLOGY IN COLOSSIANS

Christians live in the overlap of two ages—this present age and that which is to come. In Jewish apocalyptic thought, the former was seen as being characterized by plagues, war, famine, and the like. It was an evil time, through which even God's people were called upon to pass, prior to the arrival of God's anointed ruler who would usher in the coming age. The New Testament teaching concerning the end-time is not unrelated to these Jewish apocalyptic conceptions, but it makes two significant modifications: first, the figure who will appear at the advent is not some unknown entity: it will be the Son of Man on the clouds of heaven, who is none other than the crucified and risen Lord Jesus Christ. Secondly, with the death and resurrection of the Lord Jesus Christ, the "coming age" has been inaugurated even while the present age continues, so that we as Christians live in the overlap of the two eons. On the one hand, as those who are in Christ, we have already participated in the world to come, the powers of the new age have broken in upon us, and we already participate in the resurrection life of Christ. On the other hand, we are still in Adam. The sufferings of this present time are still very real, even if they are not worth comparing with the glory yet to be revealed. The warfare between flesh and Spirit still continues until the last day, and we long for that final adoption, the redemption of our bodies. We know the tension that exists between the "already" and the "not yet," between the life of heaven and an existence that is still earthly.

The "already" and the "not yet" in Colossians

That tension is brought out in Paul's Letter to the Colossians, although in this apostolic writing there is clearly an emphasis on the "already" rather than the "not yet," upon the realized, rather than the future, eschatology. In the important paragraph about "Christ in all his fullness" (Col 2:9–15), the apostle states that the readers "have been filled in him [i.e. Christ]" (v 10), *este peplērōmenoi* being a perfect tense which points to a continuing state as the result of a prior action of God. In their union with Christ, the Colossians have already come to fullness of life. Elaborating on what this means, Paul then speaks of their having died with Christ in his death, of their being buried with him in baptism, and of their having been raised with him in resurrection (vv 11–12). Somewhat surprisingly, it is asserted that the resurrection of the Colossians with Christ has already taken place (v 12, *sunēgerthēte* means "you were raised"). Similarly in chapter 3, it is declared that they "*were raised* with Christ" (v 1) and that their "life is now hidden with Christ in God" (v 3). Other instances could be cited to draw attention to this emphasis on realized eschatology, on the perspective of what has "already" been done in Christ.

It has sometimes been argued that Colossians (2:12; 3:1) and Ephesians (cf. 2:5–6), in speaking of Christians as *already raised* with Christ, are at variance with the "genuine" Pauline letters where their resurrection remains a hope for the future (cf. 2 Cor 4:14; Phil 3:11). Romans 6:5–8 is said to have particular relevance here:

> If we have been united with him in his death, we will certainly also be united with him in his resurrection. . . . But if we have died with Christ, we believe that we shall also live with him. (NIV)

It may be true that the believer's participation in the risen life of Christ finds clearer expression in Colossians 2:12; 3:1, and Ephesians 2:6 than elsewhere in Paul's letters. This is not to suggest, however, that it is absent from the earlier epistles or that someone else is responsible for the Colossians phraseology, thus giving clearer expression to the apostle's central thought than Paul himself could give! Whether we regard the future tenses of Romans 6:5, 8 as logical futures (if A is true, then B will also be true) or real ones, it is clear that in verses 11 and 13, where Paul bids his readers to present themselves as alive to God, he believes that they as Christians enjoy a new sort of life here and now. How could they be expected to "walk in newness of life" if they were still dead and buried? Further, 2 Corinthians 4:10–11 points to the experience of the resurrection in this present earthly life (cf. 2 Cor 13:4), while Galatians 2:19–20 speaks not of the future sharing of Christ's risen life but of a real sharing in the here and now of that life "in the flesh."

The differences of language may partly be accounted for because of the different circumstances that called forth the letters. In Romans 6:1, seeking to answer the question: "Shall we continue in sin that grace may abound?", the apostle asserts that the believer is no longer a slave to sin because he has been crucified with Christ. He has been freed from the dominion of this slave driver. He participates in the new life now and is to *walk* in that newness of life. The emphasis of the passage falls upon the believer counting himself dead to sin, not letting sin reign in his mortal body, presenting himself to God, and surrendering his members to him as instruments of righteousness. To have asserted that one had already been raised with Christ in the context of Romans 6 might have led to a smug self-satisfaction or triumphalism (as in the case of 1 Cor 4:8, "Already you have been filled! Already you have become rich!") because it was thought that since salvation had already been given fully and completely in the present, there was nothing left to do but to glory in it.

However, this was not the danger at Colossae. The false suggestion there was that the believers were not complete in Christ. They needed to follow a strict discipline of ritual and ascetic observance (2:16–23), and to take sufficient account of the spiritual powers, if they were to proceed along the path to perfection, to "fullness of life." Against this, the apostle asserts that the Colossian Christians had already been raised with Christ.

Further, although there is an emphasis on what has "already" been done in Christ, this is not to suggest that the perspective of the "not yet" is absent from the apostle's letter. Colossians 3:4 makes a clear, explicit reference to future eschatology: "When Christ, who is our life, is revealed, then you also will be revealed with him in glory." Jesus Christ is now enthroned in heaven at God's right hand. When he appears at the end of days at the Parousia, it will become plain that his own are with him. The day of the revelation of the *Son* of God will be the day of revelation of the *sons* [and daughters] of God. That future manifestation will take place "in glory" (v 4), an expression that has particular reference to sharing Christ's likeness and receiving the resurrection body. It was this same hope to which the apostle directed the Philippians' attention:

> Our citizenship is in heaven. And we eagerly await a Savior from there, the Lord Jesus Christ, who, by the power that enables him to bring everything under his control, will transform our lowly bodies so that they will be like his glorious body. (Phil 3:20–21 NIV)

Future eschatological references appear elsewhere in the letter. So in 3:6 where Paul urges the Colossians to put to death whatever is earthly in them, he lists five vices and then warns his readers that the eschatological, divine wrath will fall upon men and women for these things. At 3:24 slaves are urged to work for the Lord with all their heart, for they know that they will receive an eternal inheritance from him as a reward. The future dimension is, in our judgment, clearly in view in 1:22 and 28 where the presentation of every person perfect in Christ points to the time of the Parousia. The "hidden-revealed" motif and the theme of glory are both significant apocalyptic features (cf. 1:26–27), while spatial concepts ("above," "on earth") are used in 3:1–4 in the service of eschatology. In addition to these, the apocalyptic notion of a resurrection from the dead is found at 1:18 in the title ascribed to Christ, "firstborn from the dead." Even if the author is taking over traditional material, it is clear that he is giving the terminology his approval. This passage must be understood in light of Christ's primacy in resurrection, with the clear implication that others will participate in a future resurrection on the basis of his rising from the dead.

Finally, the very presence of the exhortations to the readers to "seek the things above" (3:1–4), and the need for them to let true heavenly mindedness find concrete expression and application in their "putting to death" (3:5), "putting off" (v 8), "putting on" (v 12), "being subject" (3:18–4:1), and "watching and praying" (4:2–6), show very clearly that godly behavior impinging on the future is very important in the letter. There is not a total emphasis on the "already" perspective in Colossians, as some imply. The "not yet" of personal eschatology is strongly evident, and the readers still live in the overlap of the two ages, this present age and the age to come. The warfare between flesh and Spirit still continues until the last day, and they—and we too—are urged by the apostle to press on in their Christian lives, as they long for the final adoption, the redemption of their bodies.

7

THE CHRISTIAN LIFE

Paul's epistles were the letters of a pastor written to those who were either his converts or believers for whom he had pastoral and apostolic responsibilities because they came within the sphere of his calling as the apostle to the Gentiles (cf. Col 1:24–2:5). His letters, which were substitutes for his personal presence, were occasional writings called forth by the epistolary situations and needs, both theological and personal, of the churches and their members. Recent New Testament scholarship has shown that Paul's epistles rarely had a single reason for their composition. More often than not they had a variety of goals and purposes. Especially is this the case in the Epistle to the Romans. No single reason can be isolated for its writing. The apostle appears to have had mixed aims, involving not only his own missionary plans and the progress of the gospel, but also his deep interest in the unity and welfare of Christians in the capital. Perhaps in Romans, more than anywhere else, Paul had a many-sided network of hopes and goals as he dictated his letter.

From the Letter to the Colossians, we have inferred that the churches at Colossae, Laodicea, and Hierapolis were the fruit of

Epaphras's evangelistic endeavor (Col 1:7–8; 4:12–13). As a native of Colossae (4:12), Epaphras was "a faithful minister of Christ" and Paul's representative (1:7) who had taught the Colossians the truth of the gospel. Apparently, the apostle had not visited this congregation, for most of its members did not know him personally (2:1). Nevertheless, he had a deep-seated concern for them, arising out of his apostolic responsibilities. He, therefore, writes to assure them that he has expended his energies on their behalf—through his struggles in prayer (cf. 4:12), his discussions with Epaphras about their needs, and now in the writing of this letter.

All of this was part of his wider struggle for the spread of the gospel (2:1). Paul desires most earnestly "that they may be strengthened in heart and instructed in love" in order that they might come to know Christ more fully, the very one "in whom all the treasures of wisdom and knowledge have been stored up" (vv 2–3). He was concerned about their Christian growth. Certainly, he rejoiced to see their "orderly life and the stability of [their] faith in Christ" (v 5). But he also wanted them to make progress in their Christian lives, both individually and corporately. Much of the letter, then, is taken up with issues of true spiritual growth and "fullness" of life in Christ, as distinct from the erroneous teaching peddled by those who wished to introduce their false teaching into the congregation.

In his instruction on the Christian life, the apostle, as a careful teacher, deals with both the negative and the positive, the tearing down and the building up. He writes so that "no one may deceive [the readers] with persuasive language" (v 4). He exposes the false teaching as being "a hollow, deceptive philosophy, which depends on mere human tradition, derived from the elemental powers of the world and not from Christ" (v 8), and he wants to be sure that no one "kidnaps" these dear Christian people. Paul is aware of the methods of those who had evil designs on the congregation, and he exposes them for what they really are. At the same time he builds up the readers by focusing on Christ in his fullness (cf. 2:9–15)—who he is and what he has done for his people. In the final analysis, this is the most powerful antidote to error.

We may be truly grateful for the apostle's presentation in chapters 2 and 3 because it contains some of the most profound teaching in the New Testament on the union of Christ with his people. Further, in the context of true Christian growth, there are striking implications for the believer's lifestyle, which flow from being joined with Christ in his death and resurrection. The Christian's interests, aims, ambitions—in fact, whole outlook—are to be centered on that heavenly realm where Christ reigns and where their lives truly belong. To be heavenly minded does not mean otherwordly living in the clouds; rather, it will result in the believer's being of maximum earthly use!

Its beginnings

We have already seen that the entry of the Colossians into the Christian life was due to the mighty action of God. It was he who had effected a marvelous change in their lives, reconciling to himself in an earth-shattering event, namely, Christ's physical death on the cross (Col 1:22), those who had been dead because of their sins and utterly out of harmony with him as the living God (v 21). He had delivered them from a tyranny of darkness, and transferred them into a kingdom in which his beloved Son held sway (1:13). When this message with its profoundly good news was carefully and systematically taught by Epaphras, the Colossians for their part gladly welcomed it—receiving Christ Jesus, the one at the center of the gospel, as their Lord—and committing themselves as disciples to him and his dynamic teaching (cf. 2:6–7).

Growing as Christians: divine and human action

If entry into the Christian life was due to the mighty work of God in his Son, the Lord Jesus, then continuing as a believer is because of God's working in the lives of his people, bringing them to maturity in Christ. Paul was so convinced of this that he confidently petitioned the God and Father of our Lord Jesus Christ to fill the readers with the knowledge of his will through all spiritual wisdom and understanding (Col 1:9). It was he who would empower them to live lives worthy of and pleasing to himself (v 9), for only he could enable them to bear fruit in every good work, increase in a knowledge of himself, and show endurance and patience (vv 10–11). The Colossians were wholly dependent upon Christ as the head of the whole body. From him that body with all its joints and ligaments received its supplies and, being knit together, grew according to God's design (2:19).

At the same time, the Colossians themselves had solemn responsibilities before God in relation to their own growth in sanctification. Throughout this letter imperatives are addressed to them as believing men and women and they are expected to obey these wholeheartedly (see especially the section "True heavenly-mindedness," below). There is a significant interplay between divine and human action in their progress as Christians. The apostle brings out this point succinctly in an important pivotal passage of Colossians when he interacts with the "philosophy" of the false teachers (2:6–7): "So then, just as you received Christ Jesus as Lord, continue to live in him, rooted and built up in him, established in the faith as you were taught, and overflowing with thankfulness" (NIV). The Colossians had begun the Christian life by submitting to Christ Jesus as Lord; they are now ("just as") to go on living under that lordship as those incorporated into him. What Paul means by walking or living in Christ is expanded by a series of four participles: "rooted," "built up," "established," and "abounding [in thanksgiving]." Remarkably, the first three of these are in the passive voice, so drawing attention to the divine activity: it was God who had been at work in their midst from the very beginning, and he was continuing to accomplish mighty things among them. It was he who had rooted them in Christ and was presently building them up in his Son, thereby consolidating them in the faith in which they had been taught (2:7). The readers were expected to live godly lives, understanding more and more of the consequences of Jesus' lordship in their midst; yet they could only do this because God himself was working powerfully among them.

This same interplay between divine and human action is brought out most forcibly in Philippians 2:12–13, where the apostle exhorts his readers:

> Continue working out your own salvation with all godly fear, for the one who works mightily in you is God who produces in you both the determination to work and the power to carry it out—all in accordance with his good pleasure.

As in the case of Colossians, here too the apostolic demand is awesome. However, the Philippians are not left to their own devices *because* (*gar*) God himself is powerfully working in them to achieve his gracious saving purposes in their lives. Since he has already begun a good work (of a new creation) in them (Phil 1:6), and continues it powerfully, they can be enjoined to work out their salvation with fear and trembling (2:12). With such a basis in the divine activity, Paul's dear Christian friends at Philippi are encouraged to press on with confidence to final salvation knowing that "perseverance . . . is His pure gift" (Calvin).

In defense of Christian liberty: freedom from legalism

Non-Christian persons often believe that if they order their lives by a series of pre-determined rules and regulations, then God will be pleased with the service rendered and legitimate claims may then be made upon him. These rules and ordinances may turn up in different areas of human existence: in the social, ecclesiastical, moral, and, especially, the religious spheres. A sense of achievement or even elation is felt when the rules are kept, while feelings of failure or shame are experienced if the required standards are not met. The whole enterprise is from start to finish self-centered, focusing totally upon human merit and achievement.

But it is not simply the non-Christian person who is subject to this kind of error. Christian men and women can easily drift into it. Even as a believer, it is all too possible to lapse into legalism, thinking that it would be appropriate to repay God, if only in a small way, for the gift of salvation that he has provided in his Son. Alternatively, it is thought necessary to follow rules and regulations of a religious flavor in order to grow as a Christian. The fulfillment of these requirements is not simply evidence of one's Christian faith or obedience, but is actually the means or instrument by which one is sanctified. And once again, the enterprise is self-centered!

It was a legalism of this kind that was being espoused by the false teachers at Colossae who sought to infiltrate and influence the congregation. These proponents of a deceptive "philosophy" stood in judgment of others (2:16), seeking to disqualify or condemn (v 18) the members of the church. They believed it was necessary to placate the principalities and powers, who controlled the lines of communication between God and humankind, by keeping strict legal observances, particularly in the areas of food, drink, and holy days (2:16, 21). This teaching advanced beyond Epaphras's elementary gospel, the argument ran, and the spiritual elite who wished to press on in wisdom and knowledge so as to attain completeness, maturity or "fullness" were urged to engage in these necessary ascetic practices. They were effective for receiving visions of heavenly mysteries and participating in mystical experiences. The "mature" were thus able to gain spiritual entrance into heaven and join in the "angelic worship of God" as part of their present experience (2:18).

Bad theology leads to bad practice. Just as in the contemporary scene men and women have wrong-headed notions about the character of God, believing that he would be pleased with a self-centered religion which has as its basis human merit and achievement, so at Colossae it was false ideas about the person and work of Christ which resulted in the opponents setting forth unusual aberrations on the practical side.

The Colossians are not to be impressed by those who boast of their own experiences and arrogantly pass disparaging judgments on the readers in connection with the various ordinances. In a section to be entitled "A Defense of Christian Liberty" (2:16–23) the apostle launches a series of devastating criticisms of both the advocates of the false teaching and their specious arguments. He points out that since God has divested the principalities and powers of their authority and dignity in Christ, then those who have been united in him are free from the constraints of the "elemental spirits of the universe." The evil powers are seen to be behind the false practices and regulations (2:20), and they have been defeated and publicly disgraced in Christ. To place oneself under the rules and regulations like those mentioned in verse 21 is to go back into slavery again, under the personal forces overthrown by Christ. It is tantamount to saying that Christ's death was useless. By contrast, just as death breaks the bond which binds a subject to its ruler, so dying with Christ severs the bond that bound the Colossians to the slavery of the principalities and powers.

Further, the stringent regulations of an ascetic nature in relation to matters of food, drink, or holy days, which follow from the demand for "severe treatment of the body" (v 23), are a shadow of the things that were to come. Christ and his new order are the perfect reality to which these earlier ordinances pointed. The rigorous prescriptions of the false teachers have no binding force. The reality has already come, and the things of the shadow no longer constitute a norm for judgment.

In writing to Corinth and Rome, where Christians had scruples about food and drink as well as the observance of holy days, Paul introduces the principle of Christian liberty, namely, "the strong" should go out of their way to avoid offending the tender consciences of "the weak" or scrupulous (Rom 14:1–15:13; 1 Cor 8:10). This, however, was not the issue at Colossae: the scrupulous were threatening to impose their rigid principles on the rest of the congregation. Christian liberty needed to be reasserted in light of false attempts to undermine it.

Because of their legalism, the proponents failed to recognize God's good gifts of food and drink, and his purpose in giving them, namely, that all without exception should be enjoyed and consumed through proper use. The very things covered by the taboos were perishable objects of the material world, destined to pass away when used. What is more, these taboos themselves were merely human inventions: "the commandments and doctrines of men" (Col 2:22). Paul's expression, which echoes the Greek version of the Old Testament (the Septuagint [LXX]), suggests a multiplicity of human teachings that could lay no real claim to absoluteness but stood over against the revelation of God's will. Like the taboos to which Jesus referred in Mark 7, they were human and nothing more; they frustrated the pure teaching of God with its liberating message.

Although the prohibitions (of which Colossians 2:21 contains illustrations: "Do not handle! Do not taste! Do not even touch!") had a reputation among contemporaries for wisdom in the spheres of worship, humility, and severe treatment of the body, they were without any value whatsoever. The false teachers were concerned about "fullness of life." The aim and goal of all their efforts—the observance of the strict regulations, the reverence and respect paid to the principalities and powers—was satisfaction. But all that was satisfied was "the flesh" (*sarx*). Their energetic religious endeavors could not hold the flesh in check. Rather, such self-made regulations actually reveled in the flesh.

Those who laid claim to these exalted and heavenly experiences were "puffed up" (v 18)—an expression that described a characteristic and standing danger of the Corinthians (all the other New Testament references to *phusioō* occur in the Corinthian correspondence: 1 Cor 4:6, 18–19; 5:2; 8:1; 13:4; 2 Cor 12:20). Their attitude and outlook were dominated by the flesh. They apparently claimed that they were directed by the mind. "Yes!" says Paul, "a mind of flesh!" They believed they were acquainted with divine "fullness" when all they were full of was their own pride! Worst of all, those who took the Christians at Colossae to task, using their own private religious experiences as the basis of their authority, were in fact rejecting Christ as their head, the one who is the source of life and nourishment by which his body lives, and the source of unity through which it becomes an organic whole. The advocates of the false teaching face the most serious of condemnations: they are severed from the very one who is the source of life and unity. "He is puffed up with idle notions from his unspiritual mind, and he does not hold fast to the head, from whom the whole body, nourished and held together with its joints and ligaments, grows with a growth that is from God" (Col 2:18–19). The application to the Colossians is plain: let them not be drawn off or enticed away by the appeal of the false teaching.

So, in his defense of Christian liberty, the apostle wants his readers to understand fully what God has done for them in Christ (see the exposition of vv 8–15) and to live in the light of that salvation of God. Any suggestion that Christ's death was insufficient or needed to be supplemented in order to reach "fullness" is anathema.

True heavenly mindedness

Paul does not conclude his critique of the false teaching at Colossae simply by urging members of the congregation to be free from legalism. He has indeed argued strongly in defense of

Christian liberty. But liberty may quickly turn into license. How may this deadly error be avoided? Also, it might appear from Colossians 2 that it was only the opponents at Colossae who were concerned about "the things above," that they were the only ones interested in "fullness" and the heavenly realm, true spiritual knowledge, or encounters with the mystical.

One may thus ask the question: What are the responsibilities set before the people of God who live in the overlap of the ages, between the first and second comings of Christ, and who already partake of the life of heaven while still dwelling on earth? Paul, in Colossians 3:1–4, in a short pivotal paragraph where he indicates the nature of true heavenly mindedness, presents the positive counterpart to the teaching of 2:8–23 and exhorts the Colossians to pursue those things that belong to the heavenly realm where Christ reigns: "seek the things above" (v 1) and "set your minds on the things above, not on earthly things" (v 2).

The grounds for this admonition are two-fold: first, the Colossians died to that old order with its elemental spirits (2:20), its ascetic and enslaving regulations, visionary experiences, and useless will-worship. Secondly, as those who have already been raised with Christ they now participate in his resurrection life (3:1–4). So their lives are to be different. Their interests are to be centered on Christ; their minds, aims, ambitions—in fact their whole outlook—are to be centered on that heavenly realm where he reigns and where their lives truly belong. The continuous ongoing effort required for such a cast of mind does not come automatically. That realm is to be sought diligently, and it is where Christ is, seated as king in the place of honor.

For the moment, their heavenly life remains hidden, secure with Christ in God (3:3). Their new life as Christians in Christ is not visible to others and, in some measure, is hidden from themselves. It will only be fully manifest when Christ, who embodies that life, appears at his Parousia (v 4).

The exhortations to "seek the things above" (v 1) and to "set the mind on the things above" (v 2) find concrete expression and application in the following imperatives. Four distinctive catchwords of early Christian teachings are found at the head of their respective paragraphs: "put to death" (3:5–11; also "put off," v 8), "put on" (3:12–17), "be subject" (3:18–4:1) and "watch and pray" (4:2–6). Being heavenly minded does not mean living in the ethereal realm!

In the first of these paragraphs the apostle exhorts those who died with Christ (2:20; 3:3) to put to death whatever belongs to their earthly nature (v 5). Using two catalogs of vices (vv 5, 8), similar to those found among pagan moralists and in the anti-pagan polemic of Jewish propagandists, Paul first describes five sins (v 5) which must be rejected utterly by these believers of the Lycus valley; he moves from the outward manifestations of sin ("sexual immorality") to the inward cravings of the heart ("ruthless greed"). Then the apostle exhorts them to discard their old repulsive habits of improper speech like a set of worn-out clothes (v 8).

The Colossian Christians have put on the new nature which is being renewed in the Creator's image (v 10). Within this new humanity in Christ there is no inferiority of one class to another; men and women of completely diverse origins are gathered together in unity in Christ, sharing a common allegiance to their Lord. Christ is all that matters; he permeates and indwells all members of his body, regardless of race, class, or background.

As those who have been raised with Christ, the believers at Colossae are addressed by means of privileged titles—in fact, the very terms used of Christ himself: they are "the elect of God," "holy," and "beloved" (3:12). Consequently, they are exhorted to don as garments the graces of Christ himself: "heartfelt compassion, kindness, lowliness, gentleness, and longsuffering." Each of these articles of clothing indicates how they should behave as God's elect in their dealings with others, particularly fellow-believers. As a result of their being clothed with "longsuffering," they are to show continual forbearance toward one another (v 13). Further, their relationships with each other should be characterized by mutual forgiveness. As the Lord freely forgave them, so when grievances arise they are to forgive each other. Love is the crowning grace with which the new person is to be enfolded—to put on as part of his distinctive dress—for love is the bond which produces perfection (v 14).

For those who live in the overlap of the ages, Christ's peace is to hold sway over every aspect of the readers' lives as they relate to one another; in other words, Christ himself, who is the Lord of peace, is to be present and ruling in their midst (v 15). And since the Colossians are said to have been called into the peace of Christ (that is, through the gospel), then the latter expression must also designate the realm or sphere in which the new person now lives. The readers are also admonished to let the word of Christ—the gospel message which centers on Christ—have its gracious and glorious way in their midst (v 16). If this occurs then the members of the congregation will mutually teach and admonish one another in an insightful, intelligent, and wise way. Such mutual instruction and admonition will take place in Spirit-inspired psalms, hymns, and songs as the Colossians sing praises to God with their whole being. Then, with an exhortation that is universal in its scope, covering every aspect of life (v 17), the apostle makes it plain that every activity is to be performed in obedience to the Lord Jesus and accompanied by the giving of thanks to God through him.

To those who have already been raised with Christ, and who are urged to seek the things above, the household rules (3:18–4:1) indicate how that life which is submitted to the lordship of Jesus Christ is to be expressed concretely. Perhaps the devotees of the false teaching at Colossae were indifferent to mundane and domestic affairs. If so, then Paul has to indicate to the congregation that this teaching is pernicious, and that the Colossians are to be recalled to the simple duties of family life. The apostle has already summoned his readers to "set their minds on things that are above" (3:2), for a life ruled from above where Christ is reigning is precisely a life in marriage, parenthood, and everyday work. Right behavior in these areas is the proper outworking of seeking the things above.

Paul is concerned with significant human relations within the Christian household, not abstract ordinances. The series of admonitions are addressed successively to wives and husbands, children and fathers, slaves and masters—from the closest relationship to the most distant. The admonition to wives is an appeal to free and responsible agents voluntarily to subordinate themselves to their husbands since this is entirely proper within the new fellowship of those who own Christ as Lord (3:18). The husband, for his part, is to show unceasing care and loving service for his wife's entire well-being (v 19). Christian children are enjoined to obey their parents in all things. Such obedience is all of a piece with their submission to Christ as the following words show: "for this is pleasing in the Lord" (v 20).

At the same time, parents, especially fathers, are not to irritate or provoke their children, lest the children become discouraged or think that it is useless trying to please the father within the life of the home (v 21). There should be firm guidance, not servitude (cf. Eph 6:4). Slaves who have become believers are to accept their station as slaves and to obey their earthly masters in everything (v 22). Their service is not to be superficial or performed only to attract attention; rather, Christian slaves are to serve conscientiously, out of pure motives, recognizing that as they engage in wholehearted work for their masters, so in that very action they are serving their heavenly Lord (vv 22–23). They are to keep the transcendent end in view, for their Master gives as his gracious reward an eternal inheritance of life in the age to come (v 24). Earthly masters are not commanded to free their slaves, but to treat them justly and fairly, for they owe obedience to a Master in heaven (4:1). (See a fuller discussion of slavery in the first century at the conclusion of chapter 8.)

Finally, in the concluding section of his catechetical (teaching) material (4:2–6), the apostle admonishes his readers to persist in petitionary prayer (see below) as they look forward in anticipation of Christ's return, his glorious manifestation (3:4). While they live in the interim between the ages, they are to behave wisely toward non-Christians. This will involve their being tactful, yet bold, in their Christian witness as they make the most of every available opportunity. Their time is limited, for the day of the Lord Jesus draws near.

An emphasis on thanksgiving

Before concluding our study of the Christian life in Colossians it is necessary to look in further detail at two further activities, namely, thanksgiving and petitionary prayer. In his other letters, Paul makes it clear that joyful "thanksgiving" to God should characterize the lives of those who are in Christ. In fact, one could justly argue that the regular offering of thanks to the Father is almost synonymous with being a Christian. What role in the Christian life does Paul assign to thanksgiving in Colossians? Furthermore, what special significance, if any, does he attach to prayer and intercession?

All men and women, as God's creatures who possess the raw materials of the knowledge of God, ought to render thanksgiving and glory to him (Rom 1:21). But they fail to do so (cf. the "ungrateful" of 2 Timothy 3:2, an expression which describes the character of humanity in the last days). Christians, by contrast, are to live out their lives in joyful thanksgiving because of the grace of God given to them in Christ Jesus (1 Cor 1:4). We are encouraged to give thanks "under all circumstances" (1 Thess 5:18); it should be offered to the Father through Jesus Christ as the accompaniment of every activity, being the appropriate response of those who are filled with God's Spirit (Eph 5:18–20). God's action in Christ is that of grace; our response should be one of gratitude.

In the world of Paul's day, examples from the papyrus letters show that thanksgiving to the gods was stereotyped, perfunctory, even hollow, and sprang from a sense of duty. If the worshiper was ungrateful, then it was believed the gods would not bless him on future occasions. Not so the apostle, for he mentions this subject of thanksgiving more often per page than any other Hellenistic author, pagan or Christian. Standing in the foreground of his thought, the offering of thanks to God was real, living, and vital.

Although our English word "thank" means to express gratitude to a person because of personal benefits received, and is to that extent rather self-centered, for the apostle, thanksgiving approximated to what we normally understand by "praise." It signified a thankful attitude of mind or disposition which was expressed outwardly in thanksgiving. In addition, the giving of thanks was corporate or public. By mentioning what God had graciously done in his Son, other Christians were encouraged to thank him also, and as thanksgivings abounded, so God would be glorified (2 Cor 4:15; cf. 1:11). The apostle consistently gave thanks to God for the graces he had imbued in the lives of others, particularly those in the churches of the Gentile mission.

The note of thanksgiving is struck again and again within this short Letter to the Colossians, so that the emphasis on this activity found elsewhere in Paul is, if anything, underscored even more forcibly here. There were good grounds for the apostle and these Gentile Christians expressing their joyful gratitude to God (1:3, 12; 2:7; 3:15, 16, 17; 4:2). In accordance with his usual custom, he began his letter by reporting his thanksgiving to God for the faith and love of his readers (1:3–5), both of which were based on a sure and certain hope. That hope which was kept secure for them in heaven was centered on Christ himself (1:27), and was an essential element of the gospel Epaphras preached to them. By mentioning his thanksgiving (and intercessory prayer) for his readers, Paul would no doubt help to strengthen the ties of fellowship between this congregation in the Lycus valley and himself.

Within the context of his intercession for them (1:9–14; see below), Paul prays that the Colossians, as one of the hallmarks of their living a life worthy of the Lord and pleasing him in every way, might joyfully give thanks to the Father (vv 11–12). There was justification for their doing so, because he had already fitted them for an eternal inheritance, delivered them from a tyranny of darkness, and transferred them into a kingdom where his beloved Son held sway (vv 12–13). Furthermore, under that rule of the Lord Jesus Christ, there were redemption and the forgiveness of sins (v 14), blessings which were good news indeed for the Colossians who had been alienated and were at enmity with God. By indicating that he prayed for his readers along these lines, the apostle is clearly signaling to them as to what he considers important for their Christian lives. Knowing that Paul was interceding for them in this way would no doubt have encouraged the Colossians to heed this indirect exhortation.

The remainder of the thanksgiving references in the letter are direct exhortations. In Colossians 3:17, the comprehensive nature of thanksgiving is stressed. The offering of thanks to God as Father is to be the accompaniment of every activity of those who have been called into the body of Christ. A "thankful attitude" (3:15) is inculcated in those who are in this new relationship to God—an attitude that will show itself outwardly and corporately as they "sing psalms, hymns, and spiritual songs 'with gratitude'" (v 16). The parallel injunction in Ephesians 5:20 stresses the continuity of the thanksgiving ("always"), its corporate nature—which need not be restricted to worship in church (cf. v 19)—and the fact that it is the proper outcome of those who are filled with the Spirit (v 18). In Colossians 2:7, those who have received Christ Jesus as Lord for their tradition are to continue in him "abounding in thanksgiving." In this context, firmness and strength of faith, coupled with thanksgiving, describe the Christian way of life. As might be expected in these exhortatory contexts, thanksgiving is conjoined with petitionary prayer (see below). So the Colossian Christians (4:2) who are exhorted to persevere in this latter activity are to match it with the giving of thanks, that is, their petitions are to be accompanied by thanksgivings.

For the Colossians, then, offering joyful "thanksgiving" to God the Father was to characterize the Christian lives; they had much for which to be grateful to God, for he had acted mightily in his Son on their behalf.

The place of prayer and intercession

If it is impossible to deal satisfactorily with Paul's teaching on "The Christian Life" without determining the significance he attached to thanksgiving, then it is no less true of prayer, especially petitionary prayer. Even a cursory glance at his letters shows that the apostle regarded the mutual intercession of himself and his converts as of paramount importance. We find scattered throughout his epistles, often at significant points, numerous examples of wish-prayers, prayer reports, and personal requests for intercession, apart from instances of specific teaching and exhortation on this subject. He recognized that the Christian growth of his readers, as well as the furtherance of his own ministry of the gospel, was wholly dependent upon the living God, who gave generously to his children when they called upon him in prayer. As a result, Paul constantly offered petition for his converts and others for whom he had pastoral and apostolic responsibilities. At the same time, he urged his readers to support him in their prayers for, when they interceded for him at the throne of grace, they were actually cooperating with him in his ministry (2 Cor 1:11; cf. Phil 1:19). He earnestly desired this prayerful participation in his struggle for the gospel from churches which he founded, as well as from others in the Gentile mission (Rom 15:30–32 and Col 4:3–4).

A strong case could be made for regarding Paul as one of the most gifted leaders in the whole history of the Christian church: he was an apostle and a teacher, a theologian and an evangelist (a combination rarely seen today!), a deeply committed pastor who had prophetic insight, a man who had the gift of speaking in tongues (1 Cor 14:18) and, who above all, was an instrument in God's hands in the writing of Scripture. He of all people might be expected to achieve great things for Christ through his own remarkable abilities. After all, they were God-given. Yet Paul was profoundly dependent upon Christ's grace in all that he did. He stated quite candidly to the Roman Christians: "I will not venture to speak of anything except what Christ has accomplished through me in leading the Gentiles to obey God by what I have said and done" (Rom 15:18 NIV). He was prepared to boast gladly about his weaknesses, so that Christ's power might rest upon him (2 Cor 12:10). That dependence upon Christ and his sufficiency led him to present his requests to God in petitionary prayer, along with thanksgiving, and to urge his fellow-Christians to do likewise (Phil 4:6).

Paul was convinced that his own apostolic ministry could not be carried out effectively apart from calling upon God in prayer. He recognized that the bold and courageous preaching of the gospel was only possible in answer to prayer: "Brothers, pray for us that the word of the Lord may spread rapidly and be honored" (2 Thess 3:1), and again, "Pray also for me, that whenever I open my mouth, words may be given me so that I will fearlessly make known the mystery of the gospel, for which I am an ambassador in chains. Pray that I may declare it fearlessly, as I should" (Eph 6:19–20 NIV). A pastoral visit to the Thessalonian Christians, which had been hindered by Satan, could be made as a result of God answering Paul's intercessions (cf. 1 Thess 2:18 with 3:10–11), while a journey to Rome, which was integral to a new sphere of apostolic ministry to Gentiles but which had been repeatedly frustrated, was a matter about which he was constant, if not urgent, in his own requests to God (Rom 1:10).

Further, if Christian friends, like the Philippians, were to grow in love and discernment so that they might be mature and filled with the fruit of righteousness, then God was the one to be petitioned so that he would supply them with these gracious qualities (Phil 1:9–11; cf. 1 Thess 3:12). And if the Colossians were to understand and experience the truths later expounded in the letter sent to them, so enabling them to combat the errors of the false teachers who were making their way into the church, then the illumination of the Holy Spirit was necessary. The Letter to the Colossians is part of Holy Writ. Yet the mere reading of this to the congregation, when it gathered at Colossae, neither guaranteed nor compelled the right kind of response to the apostolic teaching. Consequently, Paul prayed that God would fill them with "the knowledge of his will through all spiritual wisdom and understanding" so that they might "lead a life worthy of the Lord and please him in every way" (Col 1:9–10).

Finally, since it was God himself who could make Paul's Christian friends ready and blameless for the Second Coming of the Lord Jesus, intercessions were to be offered to him so that he might complete the work of grace he had begun in their lives (1 Thess 3:13; cf. Phil 1:10).

Thus, the apostle, knowing that God would respond to his petitions generously and liberally, brought *each phase of his ministry* to the throne of grace in prayer—from the initial preaching of the gospel, through the pastoral follow-up, to the converts' faithfulness and blamelessness on the final day. Petitionary prayer was an essential weapon in the apostolic armory. Paul knew that he was engaged in a deadly spiritual warfare and needed to make use of the whole armor of God: he heeded his own advice to "Pray at all times in the Spirit, with all prayer and supplication" (Eph 6:10–20, esp. v 18).

When we look in detail at the Letters to the Colossians and Philemon, we encounter this same broad range of prayer material. In relation to the needs of the whole congregation, as well as those of Philemon and the church that met in his home, Paul clearly regarded prayer as vital to his ministry.

1. In accordance with his normal practice, he opened both of these letters with his *apostolic greeting* ("Grace and peace to

you from God our Father and the Lord Jesus Christ," Philem 3; cf. Col 1:2) which indicates a deep prayerful concern for these readers that they may understand and appreciate more fully the grace of God in which they stand and the relationship of peace that God has established with them. The *closing greetings* of these two letters contain a benediction for God's (or Christ's) grace, together with a request, that the Colossians might remember his bonds (Col 4:18; Philem 15).

2. Paul's *intercessory prayer* of Colossians 1:9–14 is one of the finest in his letters and, along with the prayers in Ephesians (1:17–19; 3:14–19), has served as a profound model for generations of Christians. Having reported his thanksgiving to God for the faith and love of the Colossian Christians (Col 1:3–8), he proceeds to spell out the content of his intercessory prayer for them (vv 9–14). Basically, his petition is that his readers might know God's will and have the power to do it.

The notions of "fullness," "riches," and "abundance" are frequently found in Paul's prayers. The one to whom the apostle directed his requests gave richly and abundantly: "And my God will *fully meet every need of yours* in accordance with his riches in glory through Christ Jesus" (Phil 4:19; cf. Rom 15:13; 1 Cor 1:4–5; 2 Thess 1:11; note also Jas 1:5). So here, as a pastor who is satisfied with nothing less than the Colossians' full Christian maturity, Paul earnestly asks that they *might be filled* with a knowledge (*epignōsis*) of God's will (1:9). They had already come to know (*epegnōte*, cognate with *epignōsis*) the grace of God through the gospel (v 6); he now wants them to progress in that knowledge "in all spiritual wisdom and understanding" (v 9). In his letter Paul instructs them about the dangers of the "heresy" that was making inroads into the congregation. But unless God by his Spirit imparted to them the knowledge of his will, they might succumb to its insidious teaching.

Apparently, the heretical teachers were claiming that Paul's man, Epaphras, did not teach the Colossians the full Christian message. He had only introduced them to the elementary steps, whereas they offered the fullness of truth and spiritual maturity. But, in fact, Paul and his colleagues had so taught and consistently prayed (cf. 4:12) that the Colossians might receive fullness of blessing, and he indicates in the prayer that unfolds (1:9–14) what that fullness was.

The Colossians were to live in a manner worthy of the Lord, pleasing him in every way. This involved, first of all, "bearing fruit in every good work and growing in the knowledge of God" (v 10). Fruit-bearing and increasing were marks of the gospel (v 6); they were now to characterize the readers themselves. Behavior fully pleasing to the Lord included a crop of good deeds and growth in understanding. The standards set before these converts of the Lycus valley were indeed high, and the only way they could achieve these divinely sanctioned goals was through God's glorious might. The strength that would enable them to live in such a manner, as they exercised patience and long-suffering, could only come from above (v 11). Paul's petitionary prayer thus includes this important element. And he also prays that the readers may give thanks to the Father for his mighty, gracious work in their midst (vv 12–14). There was ample basis, indeed, for such thanksgiving: God had given them an eternal inheritance, delivered them from the power of darkness, and transferred them into a kingdom where his beloved Son rules. In that domain, the blessings of redemption and the forgiveness of sins abounded.

It is clear from this prayer report, in which Paul demonstrates his profound pastoral concern for his readers, that he earnestly desired that they might grow in spiritual knowledge so as to combat the dangers facing them. Paul recognized that, apart from God's granting such wisdom, his teaching and exhortation in the subsequent words of his letter would be of no avail.

The parallel intercession for Philemon (v 6) also springs out of thanksgiving to God. As he begins his introductory paragraph, the giving of thanks to God is uppermost in Paul's mind (vv 4–5). He has received good reports about Philemon's love to all God's people, a love that arose out of his faith in the Lord Jesus. The apostle then turns directly to petition, and once more he calls upon God for the Christian growth and maturity of his friend. He earnestly desires that Philemon's generosity and liberality might lead him effectively into a deeper understanding and experience of all the blessings that belong to him—and others—in Christ. If this request is answered, then Paul may be sure that Philemon will receive Onesimus as a brother in Christ, and not be angry with him, though there may have been good reason for it.

Thus, in two major intercessory prayers (Col 1:9–14; Philem 6), Paul has focused on the central issues of the two letters and interceded for his readers—in effect, asking God to enable the Colossians to deal effectively with the dangers facing them, and for Philemon that he may respond in the appropriate way to the issue concerning his runaway slave. In each report, the apostle shows that petitionary prayer was vital for the fulfillment of his apostolic ministry.

3. Within the personal greetings and instructions of the letter (4:7–18), we encounter a further reference to prayer, namely, the mention of Epaphras's intercession for his fellow-Christians at Colossae (4:12–13). This brief prayer report also had the Colossians' fullness and maturity in Christ as its goal. They had learned the truth of the gospel from Epaphras (1:7). As a native of Colossae, Epaphras had been the evangelist in his home town, as well as at Laodicea and Hierapolis, apparently having been sent there by Paul. Epaphras was in the same service of the Lord Jesus as was Paul (he is called a "fellow-servant"), and the apostle in this report goes out of his way to stress the close correlation between his own ministry and that of Epaphras. Both are involved in the same struggle for the gospel. Both are committed to urgent intercessory prayer as part of that struggle (1:9–11), while both are concerned for the full, spiritual maturity and completeness of the Christians at Colossae and in the Lycus valley generally (cf. 1:28; 2:1–5).

Epaphras was intimately acquainted with the affairs of the congregation. Perhaps he, as no other, knew of the destructive nature of the false teaching and thus responded in regular, urgent intercession. Epaphras was engaged in the same struggle for the spread of the gospel as Paul, and this found particular expression in urgent and unceasing intercessions for his countrymen. In words similar to the apostle's own prayers, the evangelist from Colossae urgently requested that his friends "may stand firm in all the will of God, mature and fully assured" (4:12 NIV).

4. Finally, in a short paragraph (4:2–6) that concludes the exhortatory section of the letter, Paul urges his readers to persist in petitionary prayer (a point stressed by *proskartereite*, "devote yourselves," on the one hand, and *grēgorountes*, "being watchful," on the other). Particularly is the cry *Maranatha* ("Our Lord, come") to be on their lips and in their hearts as they look forward in anticipation to Christ's glorious manifestation (3:4). The apostle, we have seen, regularly remembered the Colossians in his prayers (1:3, 9–14). He now requests them to bring his coworkers and himself before the throne of grace, praying that God would open a door for the gospel message, and thus for the messenger, which might well involve his release from prison. As apostle to the Gentiles, Paul has the great privilege of making known the previously hidden divine purpose, that purpose by which Gentiles are incorporated into the Messiah on an equal footing with Jews, and he now asks that the Colossians might pray to the living God to enable him dutifully to set forth that divine mystery fully and clearly (Col 4:3–4).

PHILEMON

8

THE LETTER TO PHILEMON

The Letter to Philemon is the shortest of the Pauline epistles, and is more closely related to the ordinary private and personal letters of the time—related in a way that others addressed by Paul either to communities or groups of communities are not. This does not indicate, however, that it is simply a piece of private correspondence; like the apostle's longer letters, it is an instrument of early Christian missionary work and a substitute for Paul's personal presence.

The occasion of the letter

The recipient of this letter is Philemon, who is described as Paul's "beloved co-worker" (v 1). Others mentioned in the salutation are Apphia, who was probably Philemon's wife, Archippus, Paul's fellow-soldier (and possibly the son of Philemon and Apphia), and the community (*ekklēsia*) that assembled in Philemon's house (v 2).

The occasion of the Letter to Philemon can be inferred from its contents, though not all the details are clear. A slave named

Onesimus had wronged his owner, Philemon, who was a Christian living at Colossae (vv 1–2; cf. Col 4:9, 17). Onesimus had in some way come into contact with Paul, perhaps as a fellow-prisoner. He may have sought refuge in Paul's company, because he had heard his name mentioned in the house of his Christian master.

The precise nature of Onesimus's offense is not certain. It is usually assumed on the basis of verse 18 that he had stolen his master's money and then absconded. But it is equally possible that the words, "if he has wronged you or owes you anything," simply indicate that Onesimus had been sent to fulfill some commission, and had overstayed his leave.

In the Roman world of Paul's day, slaves sometimes ran away. They joined groups of robbers, attempted to disappear in the subcultures of large cities, tried to flee abroad and be absorbed into the work-force, or sought asylum in a temple. Onesimus, however, by whatever means, came into contact with the imprisoned apostle. Paul took an interest in him, and Onesimus was later converted to the faith (v 10). The apostle clearly developed a great affection for him (cf. v 12), and benefited from his ministry (vv 11, 13). He would dearly have wished to keep Onesimus with him so that he might take Philemon's place at his side in the service of the gospel. But he had no right to retain Onesimus: this would not only have been illegal according to Roman law; it would also have involved a breach of Christian fellowship between himself and Philemon.

So Paul sent Onesimus back to his master, Philemon, together with the accompanying letter. Using gentle language and carefully chosen words, Paul requests that Philemon might welcome his slave just as he would receive himself (v 17), that is, as a "beloved brother" (v 16). He does not want the reconciliation between master and slave to collapse because of any demand for compensation, so he asks that any outstanding debt arising from Onesimus's action might be charged to his own account. After all, did not Philemon owe his very self to Paul, since the latter was responsible for his conversion (v 19)? The decision is to be Philemon's entirely, so Paul refuses to issue him any command or to press him in such a way as to suggest coercion or any intrusion (v 14). The apostle is confident that his friend will respond in a godly way, and believes that he "will do even more than I say" (v 21). These words are tantalizing but, as we read between the lines, we conclude that the "more" of which Paul speaks is Philemon's willingness to return Onesimus to Paul for the service of the gospel (v 21).

In his bold request for Onesimus, Paul uses gentle language (vv 8–9) with its tones of entreaty, then leads on to an appeal for Philemon's willing cooperation and consent (v 14), and finally, with his promissory note, indicates his willingness to accept any liability Onesimus may have incurred (v 19). Although it has been suggested by some that the letter was to be read aloud in the church at Colossae for the purpose of putting pressure on Onesimus's owner so that he would capitulate to Paul's demand, the evidence is decisively against this. To start with, the body of the letter is addressed to an individual, Philemon, not the whole church at Colossae; Paul consistently uses the singular "you" to refer to Onesimus's owner alone. The inclusion of other Christians' names in the salutation (vv 1–2) and benedictions (vv 3, 25) is due to Paul's courtesy. Further and most significantly, Paul exercises great discretion and tact as he graciously makes his request. It is a total misunderstanding to suggest that he asserted his apostolic authority and made Philemon accede to his demands. This is the very thing Paul does not do (see vv 8–9). Finally, a reasonable inference from the preservation of the letter in the canon is that Paul's request to Philemon concerning Onesimus was granted. Otherwise, the letter would probably have been destroyed.

Philemon's generosity and Paul's request

This letter, written in connection with the slave, Onesimus, reflects Paul's warm, personal relationships with his dear friend and fellow-worker, Philemon. Paul affectionately commends his colleague for his generosity and commitment to himself and the ministry of the gospel. On the basis of these, he is able to present his request to Philemon, albeit in a gracious and courteous way.

The movement of the Letter:

1. In his introductory greeting, Paul expresses his deep, prayerful concern for Philemon and his friends, that they may understand and appreciate more fully the grace of God in which they stand, and the relationship of peace that God has established with them (vv 1–3).

2. As he remembers Philemon in his prayers (cf. vv 4–7), Paul is able to express his grateful thanks to God for his friend's Christian faith and love which were actively demonstrated to all of God's people. He had received current reports, no doubt from Epaphras and possibly from Onesimus, about Philemon's good standing as a Christian (vv 4–5). Paul's thanksgiving leads on directly to his petition—an intercession concerning Philemon's generosity (v 6). It is that his liberality (*koinōnia*) might lead him effectively into a deeper understanding and experience of every blessing that belongs to him "in Christ." These Christian blessings of which the apostle has spoken do not belong to Philemon alone. They are for all who have been incorporated "into Christ" and include Paul himself. Then, using the language of direct address ("brother," v 7), the apostle tells his friend why he has been refreshed and comforted by him. The latter's love had been concretely shown to the Colossian Christians, and Paul can identify with these fellow-believers (some of whom he knew: Col 2:2), for he asserts that the "joy and comfort" given to them is received also by him.

This whole passage (vv 4–7) prepares the ground for the request that is to follow, a point that is evident, not only in the general emphasis of the passage but also in the repetition of specific words, from the thanksgiving paragraph throughout the rest of the letter, e.g., "love" (v 9), "fellowship" (v 17), "good" (v 14), and "refresh" (v 20). The apostle had commended the generous character of the slave owner's relationships with his fellow-Christians. He too had been encouraged by this love, and he now has a favor to ask. It is the request about Onesimus—the subject which prompted the writing of the letter.

3. In the body of his letter, which is a carefully constructed paragraph (vv 8–20), Paul makes his request for Philemon's slave, Onesimus. He weighs his words carefully as he gradually leads Philemon to the actual request. He begins with a brief description of his situation (vv 8–12), indicating that although he has boldness or openness in Christ to command Philemon to do what is proper for him as a Christian in the circumstances concerning Onesimus, he does not intend to enforce compliance with his word. Instead, he bases his appeal on other grounds, namely, Philemon's love. Precisely because he knows of Philemon's kindness and generosity in the past, he is able to entreat him, and he looks forward to his colleague's love being shown once again, this time in connection with Onesimus. Paul's request comes as one who is both an ambassador and slave of Christ Jesus, and his plea is on behalf of his child, Onesimus, who was converted through his ministry while he was in prison (vv 9–10).

The apostle indicates how very dear he has become to him by stating that he is sending back the one who is his very heart (v 12). As a Phrygian slave—and they were proverbial for being unreliable and unfaithful—he had previously been useless to Philemon. But a great change had occurred and Paul describes this by a "once-now" contrast. A mighty transformation had occurred when Onesimus was converted to the Lord Jesus Christ; he might now be called "useful," a description that truly fits his name, for Onesimus means "profitable" or "useful" (v 11).

Paul then looks back to the time when Onesimus came to him seeking refuge. And after his conversion, he would dearly have loved to retain Onesimus with him so that he might take

Philemon's place in assisting him in the preaching of the gospel, especially as he was in prison on its account (v 13). But not only would it have been illegal according to Roman law for Paul to act in this way; it would also have involved a breach of Christian fellowship between himself and Philemon. He would do nothing without the latter's consent or act in such a way that might suggest coercion or an intrusion into Philemon's decision (v 14).

Further, if Paul had detained Onesimus, he might well have acted contrary to God's hidden purpose. He puts forward this suggestion modestly, since he is not presuming to be acquainted with God's designs: "Perhaps he [i.e., Onesimus] was separated from you for a little while so that you might have him back forever" (v 15). The words are chosen carefully, designed to turn Philemon's attention from the individual wrongs he may have incurred to God's providence which has made these wrongs work for good (cf. Gen 45:4–8).

At the conclusion of the body of the letter (vv 17–20), the apostle spells out the content of his request: "welcome him as you would welcome me" (v 17). Although Onesimus has just been referred to as a "slave," this is immediately qualified by means of an antithesis: he will be far more than a slave to his master—a beloved brother. And it is precisely in this category that Philemon is urged to receive Onesimus. Paul is not asking that he be received back as a freed man, or that Philemon is to free him immediately on his return. By being spoken of as a "brother," Onesimus is addressed in exactly the same way as Philemon (cf. vv 7, 20): he, too, has been incorporated into the body of Christ. Accordingly, the relationship between the two men is deepened so that, in a sense, the terms "master" and "slave" are transcended, and their behavior ought to be conducted in light of their belonging to the same Lord. Onesimus's freedom may have a positive value; but finally it is of no ultimate significance to him as a Christian as to whether he is a slave or free. In the end, what matters is to have accepted God's call and to follow him (cf. 1 Cor 7:21–24).

So that there may be no hindrances to Philemon's favorable reception of Onesimus, Paul urges that any outstanding damages resulting from the latter's flight be charged to his own account (v 18). "Put that on my bill" (v 19) are the words of the apostle's promissory note to which he adds his own signature. Although he is rather hesitant to mention it, because Philemon himself had been converted through Paul's ministry, he owes the apostle his own spiritual life and this is a far greater debt than Onesimus has incurred, and for which Paul is willing to be responsible.

The message is plain. Philemon will understand that Onesimus has experienced the same grace and mercy of God as when he was converted. He is a brother in Christ and should be received as such. Philemon is not to be angry with him even though there may be good grounds for it.

4. As he concludes his letter (vv 21–25), Paul expresses his confidence that Philemon will be obedient to the will of God. He has prayed to that end, and there has been clear evidence of Philemon's obedience in the past, demonstrated so concretely in his continuous generosity as he has refreshed the hearts of the saints (v 7). As Philemon is obedient to the will of God, so Paul knows that he "will do even more than I say" (v 21), a tantalizing expression which we think refers to Philemon's willingness to return Onesimus to Paul for the service of the gospel. Finally, Paul shares his hopes to come in person and visit Philemon; if this occurs, it will be because God has graciously answered the prayers of Philemon and the other members of his household (v 22).

Slavery in the first century A.D.

The Letter to Philemon brings into focus the issue of slavery[7] in the New Testament period, and particularly in the early Christian church. By the first century A.D., almost a third of the population of the Roman empire, at least in the large cities, were slaves. Several factors account for this high proportion. Before the New Testament period many had become enslaved through capture in war, or kidnapping by pirates. After the death of the Emperor Augustus (A.D. 14), and by the time of the New Testament, the majority of slaves had been born into this position. Also, large numbers of people sold themselves into slavery for various reasons, such as better integration into Roman society, and a more secure existence than one could gain as a poor, freeborn person.[8] Further, unwanted newborn infants were "exposed" or thrown away, and, if found alive, were often raised as slaves, while Greek and Roman parents occasionally sold their children into slavery.

1. The social status of slaves

According to Roman law a slave was a *res*, that is, "a thing" and was treated like chattel to be owned. Slaves had no right to contract themselves in marriage, to inherit, or to represent themselves in court. They would often be more severely punished than freeborn persons for committing the same crime; however, slaves were protected by law from extreme cruelty by their masters.

Strictly speaking, slaves did not belong to one particular social class in Roman society. This is because their social status depended, to a large extent, on the status of their owners. While for many slavery meant living at the lower end of the social spectrum, some were well educated, having been raised and given a good education at their master's expense. A slave was not expected to wear distinctive clothing, and neither race nor roles performed in society distinguished slaves from freed persons or those who were freeborn.

In Greco-Roman families, slaves performed a wide range of functions: they served as cooks or cleaners, tutors, physicians or nurses, and even as managers of the household. In the business world, some slaves performed menial tasks, while others rose to positions of importance as managers of estates and ships, administrators of personnel, and executives with significant decision-making powers. Under Roman and Jewish law slaves could own property (including other slaves), which could then be used for purchasing their legal freedom.

As we have noted, capable slaves were often given an excellent education at their masters' expense, and as a result, some became famous philosophers (Epictetus, for example), teachers, administrators, and physicians. In fact, it has been suggested that: "These slaves and former slaves formed the broad 'class' of intellectuals of the 1st century."[9]

Slaves did not have to wait for their freedom before establishing friendships with their owners or other free persons, nor were they prevented from becoming members of clubs or religious organizations simply because of their legal status.

2. The freedom or manumission of slaves

Unlike slavery in the New World of the seventeenth to nineteenth centuries, Greco-Roman slavery was not a permanent condition. It was rather, a temporary phase of life, and slaves during the first century A.D. could usually count on being set free by the age of thirty. On occasion, whole households of slaves were freed , particularly after the deaths of their owners. Manumission was practiced generously, sometimes in order to further the interests of the owner and to keep the system functioning. In many cases, slavery was preferred to freedom because it offered security and sometimes good positions in a household.

Slaves who owned property—which was under their control—usually sought to increase it, thus enabling them to purchase their legal freedom at a later date and establish a secure existence as freed persons.

3. The abolition of slavery

The main lines of first-century slavery, which were woven into the legal and economic fabric of Roman society, had been fully developed at least a century earlier. And although there had been major rebellions in the Mediterranean area against a range of injustices, none of these uprisings, which occurred during 140–70 B.C., was motivated by the intention to abolish the institution of slavery. No revolutionary social programs intended to change the legal or economic structures.

Slaves controlled the large-scale production of the empire, in both the cities and the countryside, although freeborn persons dominated small-scale farming and trading. The household (*oikos*) played a significant role in the economy of the Roman empire, and slaves were central to the proper functioning of these households. In such an economic context it was virtually impossible for anyone to conceive of abolishing slavery as a legal-economic institution. Such an abolition would have resulted in widespread instability, and would not have benefited those for whom such a drastic step had been taken.

The New Testament and slavery

No New Testament writer comments on the origins of slavery. Also, no theological support for slavery, or justification for human beings owning other human beings, is presented in the New Testament, although direct evidence (including the Letter to Philemon) reveals that some early Christians were slaves and others were owners of slaves.

From the "household table" of Colossians 3:18–4:1 (cf. Eph 6:5–9; 1 Cor 7:21–24; 1 Tim 6:1–2; Titus 2:9–10; 1 Pet 2:18–21), the apostle makes the following points:

1. Slaves are involved in "serving Christ" (3:24);
2. Owners have a "master in heaven" (4:1);
3. God deals impartially with both master and slave;
4. Both are bond-servants of Christ.

In 1 Corinthians 7:21–24, Paul mentions, not the wider issue of slavery but, the possibility of the manumission of Christian slaves. Although the exact meaning of Paul's admonition is disputed, with many writers claiming that the apostle is urging Christians to take their freedom, it is more likely that he is exhorting the Christian to live according to "the new identity in Christ (the 'calling') that has become more fundamental than any social, legal, or religious status."[10]

The Letter to Philemon does not specifically address the broader question of slavery. Rather, in his carefully chosen words of verses 16 and 17 ("no longer as a slave, but as one who is much more than a slave, as a beloved brother . . . receive him as you would receive me") Paul is dealing with the issue of brotherly love in the body of Christ. He wants Onesimus to be welcomed back as a Christian brother and treated as he himself would be. There may also be the further thought that Paul does not want Philemon to delay Onesimus's manumission because of his misdeeds (v 18).

Onesimus, as well as Philemon, had been incorporated into the body of Christ, and as a result, the relationship of slave to owner within the framework of existing structures is to be conducted in light of belonging to the same Lord. The relationship between the two men is deepened so that, in a sense, the terms "slave" and "master" are transcended. While Onesimus's earthly freedom may be rightly desired and valued, this is not the significant issue. What finally matters is that Onesimus accept God's call and follow him (cf. 1 Cor 7:21–24 and Philem 16), whether he is a slave or not. Thus, it has been suggested that the Letter to Philemon is moving in the realm of personal relationships where the institution of slavery could only wilt and die.

Whether this final observation is true or not, those who confronted slavery in the New World of 17th–19th centuries A.D. grappled with an institution that differed from its first-century counterpart in a number of important respects. Greco-Roman slavery was a temporary, rather than a permanent condition, and many slaves could count on being set free by the age of thirty, if not earlier. Others were able to redeem themselves by paying all their debts. Also, racially motivated slavery was rare in the period prior to the New Testament. Members of a nation conquered by the Romans in war may have belonged to the same race. But their enslavement was occasioned by military conquest, not racial origin.

Further, a slave's social status could vary enormously, depending on his master's social position. While many slaves lived in wretched conditions, some, as we have seen, did rise to positions of importance. Finally, slaves in the first century A.D. wore no distinctive clothing and did not belong to one particular race. Thus it was not possible to distinguish them easily from freedmen or freeborn persons.

Thus, because of these differences, the opponents of slavery in the New World, who looked to the Bible for guidance, had to take into account, not simply Paul's letter to Philemon and his statements in Colossians 3 and 1 Corinthians 7 (which, as we have noted, said little about the institution), but also wider theological principles, including a Christian doctrine of humanity as made in the image of God.

NOTES

1. See F. O. Francis and W. A. Meeks, eds. *Conflict at Colossae* (SBLSBS 4. Missoula, Mont.: Scholar's Press, 1975), 163–95.

2. J. A. Fitzmyer, "The Gospel in the Theology of Paul," in *To Advance the Gospel* (New York: Crossroad, 1981), 149–61.

3. P. T. O'Brien, "Thanksgiving and the Gospel in Paul," *NTS* 21 (1974–75), 144–55.

4. G. Bornkamm, in *Theological Dictionary of the New Testament*, Vol. 4, ed. G. Kittel (Grand Rapids: Eerdmans, 1967), 814–15.

5. E. Lohse, *Colossians and Philemon* (Philadelphia: Fortress, 1971), 59.

6. P. Minear, *Images of the Church in the New Testament* (London: Lutterworth, 1961), 28, 213, together with his later article, "Idea of Church," in *The Interpreter's Dictionary of the Bible*, vol. 2, ed. G. A. Buttrick (Nashville: Abingdon, 1962), 607–17.

7. See S. S. Bartchy, *First-Century Slavery and 1 Corinthians 7:21* (SBLDS, 11. Missoula: Society of Biblical Literature, 1973), and his article, "Slavery in the NT," *The International Standard Bible Encyclopedia*, vol. 4, ed. G. W. Bromiley and others (Grand Rapids: Eerdmans, 1988), 543–46.

8. S. S. Bartchy, *Slavery*, 45–48.

9. S. S. Bartchy, *ISBE* 4, 544.

10. This is one of the main points of Bartchy's thesis.

NOTES

[illegible]

SELECT BIBLIOGRAPHY

Barrett, C. K. *From First Adam to Last. A Study in Pauline Theology*. New York: Scribner's, 1962.

Bartchy, S. S. *First-Century Slavery and 1 Corinthians 7:21*. SBLDS, 11. Missoula, Mont.: Society of Biblical Literature, 1973.

Best, E. *One Body in Christ. A Study in the Relationship of the Church to Christ in the Epistles of the Apostle Paul*. London: SPCK, 1955.

Brown, C. ed. *The New International Dictionary of New Testament Theology*. 3 vols. Grand Rapids: Zondervan, 1975–78.

Bruce, F. F. *The Epistles to the Colossians, to Philemon, and to the Ephesians*. NICNT. Grand Rapids: Eerdmans, 1984.

_________. *Paul. Apostle of the Free Spirit*. Exeter: Paternoster, 1977. American Edition, *Paul. Apostle of the Heart Set Free*. Grand Rapids: Eerdmans, 1977.

Caird, G. B. *Paul's Letters from Prison (Ephesians, Philippians, Colossians, Philemon) in the Revised Standard Version*. London and New York: Oxford University Press, 1976.

Doty, W. G. *Letters in Primitive Christianity*. Guides to Biblical Scholarship, NT Series. Philadelphia: Fortress, 1973.

Fitzmyer, J. A. "The Gospel in the Theology of Paul," in *To Advance the Gospel*. New York: Crossroad, 1981, 149–61.

Francis, F. O. and Meeks, W. A. eds. *Conflict at Colossae*. 2nd ed. SBLSBS 4. Missoula: Scholar's Press, 1975.

Gibbs, J. G. *Creation and Redemption. A Study in Pauline Theology*. NovTSup 26. Leiden: Brill, 1971.

Kim, S. *The Origin of Paul's Gospel*. WUNT, 2nd series, 4. Tübingen: Mohr, 1981. American Edition: Grand Rapids: Eerdmans, 1982.

Lohse, E. *Colossians and Philemon*. Tr. from 14th German ed. Hermeneia. Philadelphia: Fortress, 1971.

Lucas, R. C. *The Message of Colossians and Philemon: Fullness and Freedom*. The Bible Speaks Today. Leicester: Inter-Varsity, 1980.

Martin, R. P. "An Early Christian Hymn (Col. 1:15–20)." *EvQ* 51 (1979), 156–62.

__________. *Colossians: The Church's Lord and the Christian's Liberty*. Exeter: Paternoster, 1972. American Edition, Grand Rapids: Zondervan, 1973.

__________. *Colossians and Philemon*. NCB. 3rd ed. Grand Rapids: Eerdmans, 1981.

Minear, P. *Images of the Church in the New Testament*. London: Lutterworth, 1961.

Moule, C. F. D. *The Epistles of Paul the Apostle to the Colossians and to Philemon*. Cambridge: University Press, 1962.

O'Brien, P. T. "Col. 1:20 and the Reconciliation of All Things." *RTR* 33 (1974), 45–53.

__________. *Colossians, Philemon*. WBC 44. Waco, Tex.: Word, 1982.

Ridderbos, H. *Paul. An Outline of His Theology*. Eng. tr. Grand Rapids: Eerdmans, 1975.

Schweizer, E. *The Letter to the Colossians: A Commentary*. Eng. tr. Minneapolis: Augsburg, 1982.

Tannehill, R. C. *Dying and Rising with Christ. A Study in Pauline Theology*. BZNW 32. Berlin: Töpelmann, 1967.

Wright, N. T. *Colossians and Philemon*. TNTC. Grand Rapids: Eerdmans, 1986.

INDEX OF SCRIPTURES